Affiliate Mark
For Beginners

The most popular way to make money online fast.
You look for a product that you like,
promote it to others and earn a part of the profit
from each sale that you make.

By : "Santiago Johnson Smith"

TABLE OF CONTENTS [AFFILIATE MARKETING FOR BEGINNERS]

INTRODUCTION

When it comes to going into business online, one of the easiest and most lucrative methods is through Affiliate Marketing. This is because becoming an affiliate marketer requires no experience, no website and simple promotional techniques that will convert prospective buyers into customers.

For the relative newcomer, affiliate marketing offers a planned method and blueprint to begin making sales online. There are a multitude of different opportunities, niches and markets to choose from. A person can become an affiliate for just about anything from digital products to flowers and everything in between.

In this book, we will cover the basics of affiliate marketing to give you an idea of where to start, how to get started and what websites are good to work with.

We will then move into how to become a profitable affiliate in 60 days or less, becoming an affiliate insider and some advanced techniques that if applied properly will take your earnings to the next level.

This book is not the end all in affiliate learning; instead, it is a good step-off point that will lead you to other books that will expand your horizons and earnings.

By the time you finish reading this book, you will be able to implement a concrete plan that will get you into earning money quickly and easily. These techniques have worked for a long time, and they work consistently to earn money from affiliate marketing if followed.

If you are already familiar with affiliate marketing, this book will give you new techniques to add to your marketing arsenal so that you can increase your affiliate earnings and expand on the methods that you use in order to be successful.

So, without further ado, let's get started on our journey to affiliate profitability!

Section I - What Is An Affiliate?

Basics of Affiliate Marketing

The concept of affiliate marketing is a variation on the outside sales position except that it all happens in cyber-space, and there is no door-to-door component. Think of yourself as the salesman, one of many, for a specific product or service and you've mastered the basics of what is an affiliate.

People have all kinds of products and services that they want to sell online.

Part of the process to become successful is to have a large amount of traffic that is interested in what you have to offer. The way you can accomplish this is by having salesman or affiliate promote your products. When a sale is made, you share the earnings with your affiliate/salesman through commissions.

Successful affiliates make a good living by promoting products and services of other vendors in order to make that commission.

For the purposes of this book, I will focus on one of the easiest affiliate networks to get started – Clickbank and list the others with a brief look at the larger networks. Once you learn how an affiliate network like Clickbank works, you will be able to expand that to other larger networks that have a myriad of different products and services that are commissionable.

Clickbank is one of the largest, oldest affiliate networks out there online. Clickbank sells only digital products, is extremely easy to learn how to use and has a ton of vendors just waiting to snap up a good affiliate.

There is no waiting time to become a part of the Clickbank affiliate family, and the commissions are much higher than the other networks, with some commissions going as high as 75%.

Clickbank is an affiliate network in that it is a whole bunch of vendors and affiliates all working under the umbrella organization called Clickbank. Through Clickbank, products and services are bought and sold, accounting goes on within the network and commissions are calculated per product sold. Before we go any further, let's look at what you can potentially earn from one product.

For example: You promote and sell on Clickbank product called Make Money Online: Get Paid For Life!. It sounds like a pretty exciting product, right? Well, it has the highest payout of any Top 10 Clickbank Product and is the Top Converting product offer online. It pays out at a 50% commission level.

When you look at it's pitch page, it is endorsed by some pretty heavy weight people including CNBC, As Seen On TV, Small Business Opportunities, Fox News, CBS News and Readers Digest.

As an affiliate, you will earn 50% of the $97 dollar price tag, and it's repaid on a monthly basis. So, that means that for every person who signs up through your affiliate link (which we will get in a minute), you will be paid $44 each month as long as that person stays signed up.

What do you think if you simply stuck with this affiliate program and reached their magical 100 referral mark. That's $4400 per month for promoting only one product.

Are you beginning to see how lucrative affiliate marketing can be?

Think about how much you could make if you found 10 affiliate programs like this one? This is not only possible, but not that hard to accomplish if you know how.

Look on Clickbank and find 10 things that you think you might want to sell.

Make a list because as you learn more, you may want to revise it, and you may find that your choices are golden.

Affiliate Marketing 101 – The Basics

Since you are reading this book, I will assume that you are interested in making your fortune. Before you can even contemplate picking an affiliate program to join, you will need to make some basic changes in your thinking.

Change the way you think about money.

You've got to really change the way you view money and you want to begin to feel like you deserve to be wealthy. While this concept seems simple, many people don't feel like they deserve money.

As a result, their activities reflect their feelings of lack of worthiness. Instead of coming home from work and hitting the computer, reading an book, taking action on a plan, they will instead come home, sit in front of the television and time will pass.

Instead of becoming a veteran internet marketer, they will become the master of television watching.

People who feel like they should be able to make lots of money online will naturally make a lot of money online. This is not some spiritual mish-mosh, although I feel that spirituality is a part of everyone's journey. However, that is not what I'm talking about when I say people can make lots of money.

The most important thing to remember is that if you feel like you deserve lots of money, you will take the actions to make it happen.

It takes some basic things to be successful at affiliate marketing:

- ◦ Stay focused

- ◦ Pick a niche product to start with and then START

- ◦ Read this book and then take action.

- ◦ Make a schedule and then stick to it.

Start small and learn.

Avoid being overwhelmed out of the gate. You want to learn, apply it on a small level and then scale up when you feel you have the basics under control.

While you are doing this, you will start to make money. By staying focused, I mean avoid the multi-tab distractions. You can open a ton of websites in browser's nowadays. If your plan calls for answering email between a certain time and certain time, avoid reading emails before that time. Tell yourself, it will still be sitting there waiting for you at.

Research is key.

Clickbank

Clickbank has been in business since 1998, and has built their network to one of the largest retailer of digital products. With over 10,000 digital products, it is one of the premier affiliate networks. It is easy to use, easy to join and there are products in a ton of different areas from pets to electronics.

In order to earn commissions, all you need to do is take your affiliate ID and you get a link which you can use to send customers to. When they click on your link, it will record your commissions when they buy the product.

These affiliate networks generally require that you have a website that is related to the affiliate program you want to sell.

However, that's not impossible to accomplish, and you can get one at **www.blogger.com**, **www.typepad.com**, **www.wordpress.com** and the like. You can also sign up with very reasonable hosting services that provide one click installation of your blog site where you can start posting articles and blog posts related to the product or service you apply for at one of the larger networks like the ones listed below:

Clickbank is a Fast Start, Needs no website and pretty easy to be accepted into this program.

- **www.clickbank.com**

Need to have a website, makes sure that it's established with an About Us, Contact Us and Privacy page on the site. Should have a few weeks of posts at the very least.

- **www.shareasale.com**
- **www.cj.com**
- **www.rakutenadvertising.com**
- **www.amazon.com**
- **www.pepperjamnetwork.com**
- **www.datafeedr.com**
- **www.rubiconproject.com**

Wait at least 90 days before putting AdSense on your site. To ensure that you will be accepted to the AdSense program, it's best not to apply until you have an established site to show them.

- **www.adsense.com**

This serve is secondary and shouldn't be considered until you've got your sites up and running for a few months.

- **www.cpaempire.com**

Before you apply to any of the other sites, you need to have a real site. You will want to blog on the site for at least two weeks, one blog post per day.

If you aren't a writer, you will need to hire a freelancer. Go to **www.upwork.com**, **www.freelancer.com**, **www.fiverr.com** and the like to find a writer. You can hire a freelancer fairly inexpensively who will deliver you blog posts to add to your site.

Researching Your Products

Pick a niche product and start to research if it's a viable topic or subject. Whether you want to go with Clickbank products or with other affiliate products, you will need to do your research.

Finding a profitable niche should be your first type of research.

You want to have a product that is Hot! If you find a product that isn't very hot, don't expect to make any kind of money with it.

The reason I picked the Make Money Online is because it is a hot item. People are interested in the niche, and it's marketed well, presented in a professional manner, and has tools for its affiliates to use to make money.

To find out what are people looking to buy:

- Amazon Bestsellers: **www.Amazon.com**

- eBay Pulse: **www.Marketplacepulse.com/ebay/top-ebay-sellers**

- eBay Tera peak: Terapeak.com

Amazon.com Bestsellers

Amazon gives you a quick and easy way to find out what's hot and what's not on their site. It is a clear indicator of what the buying market is looking for, making it very easy for your to put yourself in the path of oncoming web traffic and make sales.

If you sign up with Amazon's affiliate program, you can sell all of the products on the site, and with the Bestsellers section, you will know for sure that certain products are selling. They even give you a Top10 list for each category so that you can use that to make articles, reviews and blog posts.

eBay Pulse Tool

This is a great place to find out what the hot products are because if a person is typing it into eBay, they are typing it into Google and Amazon. eBay Pulse gives you a real-time look at what people are looking to buy.

You can log into eBay and do a search on the completed items. It will tell you what people are selling, how many have sold and the average price. Look for items with bids, and this is a great way to get an idea of what people are looking for.

Terapeak is another great way to do things

Go to Hot Research, sort of like eBay pulse. It will give you a listing of what's hot on eBay. You can then drill down and it will give you an idea of some of the different auctions that are going on. If there are bids, this is a good item to become an affiliate for.

Hot Research > Hot Searches and then Search

Good average price above $30.00, with a good commission rate of no less than 40%, the higher the better. Also, don't go for the very high end products that are priced at above $125 dollars.

Section II – Newbie to Profitable Affiliate

Build Up To About 10 Products To Promote

As an affiliate, you will want to build up to about 10 products, so that you can mix up the top performing products and add the latest releases. While you should like what you're selling, don't be wed to it.

What may be a hot seller, may cool off and if you follow trends, you need to be able to move on. You don't want to add all these products at once, and build slowly as you get more experienced.

Because you don't want to overwhelm yourself with products, pick your products carefully. Choose popular products because you want to have top performing products.

Here are some things to remember when you are selecting products.

When you search for new products to promote from Clickbank, there are certain things that you are looking for.

First and easiest is the selection of the category that you want to work with. For instance, each affiliate products has some information that will help you makc a good decision.

The three sites you will want to use to ascertain if a product is a good seller and a possible product you will want to promote includes:

➢ Clickbank Marketplace – **www.clickbank.com**

➢ CB Trends – **www.cbtrends.com**

➢ CB Engine – **www.cbengine.com**

Clickbank Marketplace

1. Sale Price: ($/Sale) This is the amount that affiliates are earning for referring customers. The amount earned is kept by Clickbank accounting and pays out every two weeks to the affiliate.

2. Percentage of Sale: (%/Sale) This is the average percentage commissions earned per affiliate per sale.

3. Referral %: This is the percentage of sales that people you refer

4. Gravity of Product: The gravity number is important because it shows the popularity of the product over time. Every time the product is sold or a new affiliate joins and uses the link the gravity of the program will change.

CB Trends

The popularity, price and commission paid of the product is very important.

When it comes to popularity or gravity, unless you are already a Super Affiliate avoid the products with very high gravity (125+), because it means that the market will be highly competitive and the chances of you making sales will be decreased accordingly. This applies only to Clickbank and not the other commission driven organizations.

In order to find out if a product is good to add to your affiliate arsenal, you will want to check it out at CB Trends (www.cbtrends.com) which is a free service that shows visual representation of what is on the Clickbank marketplace site making it easier to understand. There are some useful tracking tools that give you an easy way to see what is happening with the products you choose including:

- ➢ Popularity of the product

- ➢ Earning per sale

- ➢ Percent per sale

- ➢ Gravity

- ➢ Referrals

- ➢ Commission

If you take the visual representation, combine it with what you see on Clickbank's Marketplace, you will have a good idea of whether the product you're thinking about promoting is a good one.

Out of the 10 products that you pick to promote over time, you will want at least 6 of them to be popular. You want to mix it up so that at least half of what you're promoting is more competitive. The rest of the products should be up and comers, those products that are newer and building in the Marketplace.

CB Engine

CB engine shows you the new products and is an excellent tool to use if you want to focus on the new product releases. If you are going to work with Clickbank, which is a good first step into the affiliate arena, CB Engine should be one of the sites you bookmark and use.

It has a Brand New Products list, re-listed products with a ton of information to help you make an informed choice about the products you want to promote. Each product, new and re-listed, have graphs and visual representations about the health and viability of the products.

There are a couple of ways to go about finding out more about the product or service you are about to promote. First, you can buy the product.

Whether it's digital or tangible, buying and experiencing the product will usually make you a better promoter. However, with 10 products, that can become a bit pricey, so you may want to buy a couple products that you can afford, and look over the sales pages only of the remainder.

When looking over the sales or pitch page, you will want to think in terms of being a prospective buyer. Ask yourself some basic questions:

➢ Does the page, headline and opening paragraph grab your attention.

➢ Is the page easy to read in terms of colors, graphics and layout of the site.

➢ Is the message being presented clear and concise and easy-to-understand.

➢ Are there highlights of important facts, headlines to break up content and pictures that are relevant to the topic matter?

➢ Does the page lead you to the logical conclusion where you want to buy the product?

All of these things are important and will make or break you when people come through your referral link. Having a page where you want to buy the product will generally translate to high sales conversions. In that way, the traffic you drive to the product site stand a higher chance of buying in the end. If the page left you with a ho-hum, whatever feeling, it is probably quite possible that visitors arriving at the site will have the same reaction. As you go about promoting your affiliate products, make sure that you keep track of the products that are converting well, and the ones that are not. When you have a hot product that goes warm and then cold, you need to be ready to get rid of it. Earlier I told you not to get attached to a product or service. This is why. You have to know when to get rid of it.

Look at the choices you first made on Clickbank and ask yourself the questions from above. Are there any products that you might want to get rid of now?

Getting Traffic To Your Site

Video Promotion

While most people will tell you to use pay-per-click advertising, article marketing and building a website, here's a shortcut method to get your started and quickly. Videos can get you into search engines fast.

Use one of these tools to get started:

- ➢ Camtasia Studio has a 30 day free trial

- ➢ CamStudio which is free and located at http://camstudio.org

- ➢ Jing that works on the Mac or PC

- ➢ Web Cam

- ➢ Sony Movie Studio

- ➢ Movie Studio 9

Now that you have a selection of products, a website or direct links to a vendor's website, it's time to promote. First, you will want to get into the video arena.

I know you probably weren't expecting that. But, people are video junkies, and if you want to get people engaged, you will need to go where the traffic goes.

Creating videos is one sure-fire way to get traffic to your site. Creating a video is not as hard as you think. It's easy and fun, and will get you into the

---

Working with Camtasia can be a little daunting, but it will pay for itself in spades if you take the time to learn how to use it.

If you need to go free Jing is the second easiest way to record from screen to video. If you're good with PowerPoint, you can create a slide show, narrate it about your site and simply read from a script. These are the easiest type of video to create, and when used correctly, they are traffic bringers.

Set your monitor resolution to 800x600 for recording. Record your videos at 800 x 600, resized to 480 x 360 with Smart Focus. You want them to be quick, and talk about the product you are promoting.

The bottom third is very important in videos. You want to tell them about your domain name or the domain of the affiliate site. If you don't have a site of your own, go to Snip-URL where you can put in your affiliate link, and it will give you an output.

For instance, if your affiliate product is for Make Money Online, and your affiliate link is **http://XXXXX.PUBLISHER.hop.clickbank.net**, your Snip-URL will be: *www.snipurl.com/makemoneyonline*

The Snip-URL can go in the lower left part of your video, and remain there for the duration. As you talk about your website, all you need to do is use SnagIt to capture pictures, which you put in your PowerPoint presentation and capture as video.

Add a couple of transitions, and you are in the video arena. These short video reviews are what you upload to all of the video sites.

Things to remember:

➢ Make sure that the name of the video is your longtail key phrase or product name plus a word like deals. (ie. Salmon deals, Rolex watch deals)

➢ Make sure that the keywords and key phrases are submitted and enclosed in quotes as well as without quotes.

➢ Make sure that you submit them with the URL leading back to your website

➢ In the information section, be sure and put your website, or Snip-URL if you don't have a website that leads back to the affiliate product.

Pay-Per-Click Advertising

If you don't have a website, landing page or place to send prospective traffic, pay per click or PPC advertising is an excellent method to drive sales via your affiliate link.

Again, you will want to use discretion so that you don't wind up losing more money than you gain in sales. The largest PPC outfit is Google. Those little advertisements that you see on people's websites, plus on the side of the search results are called PPC advertising.

Advertisers pay a set amount per click in order to appear on sites. It is considered contextual advertising, because the advertising is related to the information being presented either in the search results or on the website. For instance, you won't get an advertisement for ice cream on a site about auto parts.

Adwords & Contextual Advertising

Advertising with Google is easy and deceptive to newcomers. Easy, in the fact that it is very easy to use; deceptive because if you aren't very careful you could lose a lot of money trying to get advertising that makes you money. Here are some techniques so that you can use the Adwords system and make money.

The site is located at: **http://adwords.google.com**

You can sign up for an Adwords account by clicking the Start Now button and filling in your information. Sign up for a standard and not a starter account. Adwords is pretty easy to use. Many people will want to start out with 100s of keywords and will take everything suggested by Adwords keyword tool.

Avoid this method and stick with a few terms that are laser-focused on your product or service.

Use the Adwords keyword suggestion tool or other keyword tool like Microinches Finder, Nichebot and Keyword Elite to find about five or six terms that are tightly related to your product.

You will want these keywords/key phrases to be low competition, high traffic words. The software just mentioned are designed to find keywords like this for your product.

You will want to drill down on your keywords. For instance, if your product is about dog health, don't just look at the keywords "dog health" and dogs. Look for things like "relief for dogs from fleas", "best dog food" or go into a specific breed like "cocker spaniel health", or "best dog food for beagles".

While you will get fewer visitors based on these keywords, the ones that will arrive will be very interested in your product. When you look at products, you will want to take this into consideration as well.

List your key phrases and base your advertisement around these key phrases. You will ideally want to get them into the title of your advertisement as well as in the listing for Adwords to use when listing when your ad will appear in the search results and on people's websites.

Use the Adwords keyword suggestion tool here:

https://ads.google.com/home/

Select key phrases that are relevant but not very competitive. Remember, that although you may only get 100 visits a day from a keyword, conversion rates are 1-2%, so that will usually equal a sale.

This is why you don't want to promote a product that is much cheaper than $30. If your commission is 50% to 75% of $30, that is $15.00 to $22.50 on each sale.

It has been shown that affiliates will convert on average 1% to 2% per 100 visitors if they have done adequate keyword/key phrase research.

It will generally convert the same on a $30+ item as it does on a $15.00 product. The amount of money you earn will only change due to the commission level and price of product.

Ad Variations

When you have your keywords in hand, go to Google and search on those keywords. Put the keywords between quotation marks and watch what comes up on the right hand side. This will give you great ideas on how to word your own advertisement.

Look at what ad is in the top spot 3 spots. Look at the titles they are using and see how you can word your advertisement similarly so that you get good clickthroughs. Then when you put together your initial ad, make some variations and track how many clicks each ad is getting. Keep the ad that performs the best.

When you are just starting out with Adwords, keep your bids low. Bid as little as $0.05 cents per click where you can, and just make sure that you get on page one of the search results.

Look towards doing advertising on websites only and forego the search results, because it is counted in 1000 impressions at a price and your money can go a longer way.

URL Display and URL Actual

One nice thing to remember is that you can put your Clickbank ID and URL in the Destination URL section of the advertisement. In the Display URL, you place the actual website URL of the affiliate products vendor.

Example:

Display URL: www.makemoney.com

Destination URL:

http://xxxxxx.makemoney.hop.clickbank.net/**?tid=MAKEMONEY**

That word "?tid=MAKEMONEY" on the end of the Clickbank ID is called a traffic tracking device which allows you to track how your campaigns are going. Both Clickbank and Adwords will allow you to track your advertising campaigns so that you can make a decision about what's working and what needs to be changed.

To track within Adwords, you will need to choose a keyword that you want to track in Adwords. Click on Edit Keyword Settings. Then you have a URL that you can add a tracking ID to which in this case would be "?tid=MakMoAd1" for MAKEMONEY, Ad #1. You only have 8 letters that you can use, so whatever you decide, it should be easy to understand and decipher.

Yahoo and MSN's Adwords Equivalent Contextual Advertising

While not much is said about the contextual advertising that is available through Yahoo and MSN, it does exist. As an alternative, you might want to consider advertising through them. The same rules apply, the competition is less and you may wind up spending a lot less for the same amount of advertising.

In order to figure out if it's worth the money, you can sign up for accounts with both MSN and Yahoo pretty easily and try it out. They also run a lot of specials and give away coupons worth various amounts of money just to get you to try their service.

Yahoo PPC Service: **https://smallbusiness.yahoo.com**

Microsoft Ads: **https://ads.microsoft.com**

While these are lesser advertised, contextual advertising outlets, you can get a lot of mileage from them, and all kinds of traffic you might have missed if you focused on Google alone. Remember, being successful as an affiliate means thinking outside of the box.

Facebook and Myspace Advertising

Often overlooked and very good places to advertise are Facebook and Myspace. While I wouldn't advertise the How To Make Money Online books, they are great places to advertise other digital products.

If, for instance, one of your products is Jamorama from Clickbank, it is a "learn to play guitar online" service that is made for young people, is done totally online and would make a great Myspace advertisement.

Squidoo and Hubpages

If you don't have a website and you want to have an intermediary page that gives more information and pre-sells the product more, you can use either Squidoo or Hubpages. They are free to build, takes about 60 seconds and requires no HTML ability to use.

Tons of people build Squidoo lenses using articles that expand on the products and services that they are promoting.

In this way, a person doesn't click through your link straight to the pitch page of the vendor and only think that you are trying to sell them something.

Through the use of these intermediary sites, you can add value to the product or service with a personalized set of information that is tailored to make the product more understandable.

If you decide to build a Squidoo page for your affiliate product, most people will do a review of the product or write an article outlining the benefits of using/reading/listening to the product. In this way, it is more personal and less salesman-like.

Web 2.0 Social Networking

By using Web 2.0 social networking, you can announce and spread the word about your affiliate product. Instead of sending them directly to the vendor's site, you can use Squidoo, Hubpages and other social networking sites like Ning and Scribd.com to Presell the product through writing articles and converting them into mini websites.

Instead of advertising the vendor site, you will advertise your intermediary site and use it to list build and follow up through an autoresponder.

The easy way to list build is take a picture of one of the aWeber or GetResponse forms using a program like Snagit, and upload the picture and make it a clickable link to a squeeze page. You can build a squeeze page using Weebly.com which has a drag and drop interface that makes it extremely easy to build web pages with autoresponder forms embedded in them.

You then have people click, go to your landing or squeeze page and fill out the form. On the landing page, you can further outline the benefits of the product you are promoting.

The Advantages of Having Your Own Site

While a lot of affiliate marketers can operate without setting up a website, the benefits of doing so will become immediately apparent. First, having your own website establishes your credibility on the subject, and further lends authority to the product you are promoting.

While you can strictly use Adwords and other contextual advertising methods, having your own website is a way to add other income streams, organize and consolidate your affiliate product offerings and add other types of advertising and monetization schemes to your site.

Setting up a website is not that difficult nor is it very expensive any more. If you decide to go with your own website, there are a few things you should know in order to get started. Get your own domain name. A domain name is a unique name that identifies your website. It transforms an IP address (100.99.103.44) to something memorable – www.yourdomain.com

Having your own domain name adds to the authority of what you're writing, should be easy to remember and gives you a platform from which to write. Registering a domain name nowadays costs only about $8 to $10. Some of the best registrars include:

➢ Ifastnet.com

➢ Godaddy.com

- ➢ Namecheap.com

- ➢ Internic.com

Next, you will want to get webhosting. This is also very inexpensive. A full featured webhosting plan will cost you only about $5.00 to $10.00 per month.

- ➢ Ifastnet.com

- ➢ Godaddy.com

- ➢ Hostgator.com

- ➢ Dreamhost.com

Get an easy to use website platform. You don't need to be an HTML or Dreamweaver expert to set up a really nice site.

The platform of choice these days is Wordpress, which is very simple to setup by using Fantastico and Cpanel, and there are tons of very nice themes out there for you to use. Two other easy to use content systems are Drupal and Joomla. All three of these will build out a full site for you that has an admin interface that is easy to learn and use.

Through the use of one of these platforms, you can accomplish a number of essential things to the success of your affiliate sales:

Affiliate link cloaking: It would be nice to think that everybody is honest. However, this is not the case. As a result, you need to cloak your affiliate link so that when a person clicks through your link and buys the product, the commission goes to you.

Especially with an affiliate network like Clickbank, it is very important to cloak your original link with an ironclad decoy link that keeps the commission protected.

It will take a link that looks like a mish-mash of letters and dots and like this: **http://AFFILIATE.PUBLISHER.hop.clickbank.net** and turn it into something like this: http://yourdomain.com/product.html. It makes it both easier to read and keeps your affiliate information secret and intact.

Pre-selling: This affords you the opportunity to write or have written articles that are keyword optimized (which means that they are designed to rank highly in the search engines for specific words), traffic magnets that affords visitors the opportunity to learn more about a specific product and get more exposure that leads to eventual conversion. Pre-selling is an art that happens over time.

Ad Tracking & Analytics: While Google Adwords offers excellent ad tracking features, having a person visit your website further refines the analytics you can look at.

As a visitor explores your entire website, you are gaining valuable information about what pages they visited how long they stayed on specific pages, what links they clicked and the like. All of this information can help you refine what is on your website.

For instance, say a person arrives at your home page, goes to a page on a specific product and then goes through a link on that page to another page on your site and stays there for a long time.

If this happens over and over, you have just gained valuable information about what has caught people's interest. In that way, you can offer more of the same that is on the second page so that people are likely to return and be re-exposed to you, your products and your site.

Blogging About Specific Topics Related To Your Affiliate Product: With a website built on the Wordpress platform, you can set up certain programs called plug-ins that automatically optimize your website. What this means is that Google and the other search engine spiders will love to stop by your site and add pages to their search index.

As you get more pages into the search engines, you will rank higher. What this means is that you will have more and more visibility and in turn more traffic will visit your site over time.

Learning about keyword research and search engine optimization or SEO is one of the things that every affiliate should learn. The more you know, the better your site will become, and the better your site, the more sales you will make.

Building Quality Incoming Links To Your Site

While you don't want to go link crazy, you will want to get a number of good incoming links from High PR link sites. Be careful – don't purchase links. While you can purchase links, it's frowned upon.

Step-by-Step Checklist To Affiliate Success

With everything you've learned to date, I'll bet your head is swimming. Below is a plan that you can implement to get you started on the road to affiliate success and profit.

Get Organized!

➢ Pick on affiliate network (I suggest Clickbank because it's easy). Spend a couple of hours learning the ins and outs of how it works. Look at the gravity, sale percentages and pick some products and make some affiliate links so that you are fully familiar with how the process works.

➢ Go to CB Trends and CB Engine and make sure you understand how they can help you pick winners.

➢ Stop by the Google Adwords tool and search for about 10 keywords for each product that you pick making sure that they are low competition, good traffic keywords and key phrases.

Keep good notes about what you are doing so that you can refer back to them later.

Sign up for Pay Per Click programs

Get yourself the following Pay Per Click accounts:

- ➢ Adwords, Yahoo Publisher and MSN AdCenter accounts

- ➢ Make a decision about whether you are going to build a website or work strictly through Pay Per Click advertising.

Sign up for Clickbank

- ➢ Sign up for Clickbank and get your nickname if you didn't do that yesterday.

Go through the help files at Clickbank, Adwords, etc. so that you understand basically how each program works.

Video Training

- ➢ Make a decision about which program you want to use to make your 1 minute videos.

- ➢ Look on YouTube and search under Camtasia training. You will find a ton of videos on how to make a decent video.

➢ Check out **https://advertising.adobe.com** for free uploading of your videos after they're done. If you want more options, there is a paid portion that will allow you to submit to more video sites. Also, you can consider Traffic Geyser for maximum coverage with videos, if you have some money to spend. **www.trafficgeyser.com**

Article Marketing

Article Marketing is one of the easiest ways to get steady traffic to your website. Using good keyword/key phrase research will get you a ton of traffic as you write articles based on the results. In those article directories, you can put links back to your site and that will send traffic your way.

➢ Never submit the same article to multiple sites

➢ You need to change your article by at least 50% for each site. This is not as hard as you might think. Check out Unique Article Wizard located at: **www.uniquearticlewizard.com** on how to accomplish that.

Top 16 Article Directories

1. **ezinearticles.com**
2. **articlesBase.com**
3. **buzzle.com**
4. **pubs.acs.org**
5. **goarticles.com**
6. **articlealley.com**
7. **articledashboard.com**
8. **articlesnatch.com**
9. **ideamarketers.com**
10. **webpronews.com**
11. **amazines.com**
12. **upublish.info**
13. **isnare.com**
14. **articlesfactory.com**
15. **web-source.net**
16. **articleblotter.com**

Build Squidoo Lenses and Hubpages

➤ Get some free pages which can act as intermediary sites which you can use to pre-sell your various products by writing articles presenting the products and writing about the features and benefits.

➤ Build one Squidoo or Hubpages per article and product. Avoid combining stuff on pages, because you want to give a clear message about each product or service that you are promoting.

➢ You can build more than one page per product. Look and think about the different angles you can bring to each product or service that you are promoting.

➢ For instance: list the features and benefits in general lens, then build 4 or 5 lenses on specific sub-features where you only talk about that feature. Then, from the main lens or Hubpages, you can link to the sub-feature pages.

Autoresponders

Autoresponders are e-mail messages that are sent automatically when an e-mail arrives for a specific e-mail account. The most common example of an autoresponder is the ubiquitous "Out of Office" message sent by mail programs like Outlook and Eudora.

Web autoresponders are used by affiliate marketers to send responses to questions when they are away from the computer.

Autoresponders will answer questions, send information about a product or service. They are also key to list building which is where many affiliate marketers make backend sales by sending follow-up messages. Most web autoresponders give you unlimited auto response messages, and you can have multiple autoresponder addresses.

Autoresponders are inexpensive and are considered your silent 24/7 salesman. Two good autoresponder companies that charge around $20 bucks a month include:

> AWeber – **www.aweber.com**

> GetResponse – **www.getresponse.com**

There are many other autoresponder companies out there, and you can even get autoresponders as part of your webhosting package.

However, these two autoresponder companies offer a host of addition features and benefits that allow you to build a list super-fast.

Backend sales on follow-up messages accounts for a large part of affiliate sales. It is a known fact that people need multiple exposures to a product to convert tire-kicking to sales.

Sign Up For Web 2.0 Social Networking

It is very important to sign up for as many Web 2.0 social networking sites so that you can promote your product pages – whether they're on Squidoo, Hubpages or Weebly. In this way, you can build a steady flow of traffic to your pre-sales pages, build your list with an autoresponder form and increase sales.

The Top Sites To Sign Up For Include:

- ➢ Digg – **www.digg.com** - Digg is a website made for people to discover and share content from anywhere on the Internet, by submitting links and stories, and voting and commenting on submitted links and stories, in a social and democratic spirit. Propeller – **www.propeller.com**

- ➢ News vine – **www.newsvine.com** – News vine allows you to report on the news that you find around the net. If you have a website, News vine is a great way to get the news out about it. News vine also allows you to create your own blog, so you write articles, post reviews about products and more just like you have your own site.

- ➢ StumbleUpon – **www.stumbleupon.com** - Boasting 2.5 million users, StumbleUpon is a web browser plugin that allows its users to discover and rate web pages, photos, videos, and news articles

- ➢ LinkedIn - **www.linkedin.com** - 575 million members - a powerful tool for business networking.

- ➢ Orkut - **Orkut.com** is an Internet social networking service run by Google Now has a membership of 57 million.

- ➢ Twitter – **Twitter.com** is a free social networking service that allows users to send "updates" (text-based posts that are up to 140 characters long) via SMS, instant messaging, email, the Twitter website, or an application such as Twit terrific.

- ➢ Yahoo! 360 (a.k.a Yahoo! Days) is a personal communication portal similar to Orkut and Myspace -- it is currently in the beta-testing phase. It integrates features of social networking, blogging and photo sharing sites.

- ➢ Xanga – **xanga.com** with 40 million members. Xanga is a free Web-based service that hosts weblogs, photoblogs, videoblogs, audio blogs, and social networking profiles.

- ➢ Ryze – **ryze.com** with 25 million members. Ryze.com is a free social networking website designed to link business professionals.

Consider Building A Store

As an affiliate, you can build a store or join a program where a store is provided for you. There are a number of Clickbank-ready stores that are pre-set up. You only need to pay a onetime fee and the store will be activated in your name with your affiliate ID. So, instead of promoting just 10 products, you can promote the entire Clickbank host of vendors. There are ups and downs to this.

Pros: All the work is done for you. There is a Featured section to these stores where you can highlight the 10 products that you are actively promoting. It also gives you a quick web presence and if you don't have website building experience, everything is done for you.

Cons: Your store look just like every other person who bought the store package. Because it is built for you, it is a standardized template, so there can be hundreds, even thousands of other stores out there that are just like yours.

Set Up A Blog on a Free Site

Take a short bit of time to set up a blog on one of the free sites, or build a site and get webhosting. Whichever you decide, having a small site that is yours will go a long way towards building your credibility for the long term. Using PPC (pay per click) is fine up to a point. However, to expand and grow with products and services, having a site is essential.

Free Websites:

Wordpress: **www.wordpress.com** – You can get a blog started in less time than it takes you to read this sentence. All you need is an email address. You'll get your own WordPress.com address (like you.wordpress.com), a selection of great free and customizable designs for your blog (called themes) and 3 GIGABYTES of file storage.

There is a great deal of help and instruction to show you what to do and how to get started. Your website address would be something like https://product.wordpress.com and you can build as many of these free sites as you like. The positives of using the Wordpress.com system is that you are on a domain that has a very high page rank, lots of visitors and tons of help. Even if you've never set up a blog before, it's so easy that you can get started and not feel overwhelmed.

Blogger: Another free platform that is owned by Google is great to set up a blog on. Again, you will be a subdomain like http://product.blogspot.com, but it's free, there's no webhosting fees involved and you can set it up without any HTML, programming or web design experience. You simply pick from one of the many themes presented, and your blog is ready to go. Having a Blogger blog gets you listed in Google (since they own it), and makes it easy to get your message out there.

Joomla: Although Joomla is free, they don't have a free site where you can build on a subdomain. Joomla is an award-winning content management system (CMS), which enables you to build Web sites and powerful online applications.

Many aspects, including its ease-of-use and extensibility, have made Joomla the most popular Web site software available. Best of all, Joomla is an open source solution that is freely available to everyone.

With that said, Joomla has a ton of online help just like Wordpress; however, you will have to get webhosting and a domain name to use it.

Consider Setting Up Your Own Website

Whichever platform you decide on – Wordpress or Joomla – you will need webhosting, a domain name and it will take a bit of time to get things set up.

Most affiliate marketers tend to go with either Blogger or a Wordpress blog and self-hosting. Joomla is an option, but the learning curve is a little bit longer. So, if you're looking to get going, you might want to consider either the free services or Wordpress.

Once you decide on getting your own blog, select inexpensive webhosting. Remember, webhosting should have cPanel or One-Click setup attached to it. HostGator has cPanel and Fantastico and Dream host has One-Click. Both perform the same function – set up of Wordpress with no knowledge of MySQL, Wordpress or FTP.

This is the quickest way to get started with your blog. Once it's set up, you will need to look at article writing. If you're not a writer, check out the freelancers at Elance, Guru.com and Rent coder.

Getting Traffic To Your Site

Write down and plan the methods you are going to use to drive traffic to your website: Pay-Per-Click, Squidoo and Hubpages, article marketing, social networking and the like. Then schedule when you will be posting to your site, and posting to social networking sites.

In the end, if you follow this entire checklist and don't give up, you will begin to see sales for the products that you are promoting.

You can also add more products over time to promote, build more than one website, put up Squidoo and Hubpages highlighting your various products and services and add things like AdSense to further monetize your site.

This Manuscript Includes 2 Bonus (Two Free Books...)

HOW TO START A BLOG

Ever wondered how to start a blog and make enough money to quit your job?

With this book You can do it. Tons of people already have.

Start today you too.

(<u>BONUS 1</u>) – FREE BOOK - By : "Santiago Johnson Smith"

TABLE OF CONTENTS [BONUS 1 – FREE BOOK] - HOW TO START A BLOG

Blog Basics

Step 1: Consider Your Theme

Step 2: Giving Your Readers What They Want

Step 3: Choosing Your Platform

Step 4: Choosing Your Content

Step 5: Promoting Your Blog

Step 6: Social Networking & Book Marking

Step 7: Tying it All Together

Blog Basics

A blog is sometimes called web log or weblog. At first, they were used as a personal place, for collecting links, sharing commentary – but now; they are a valid and VALUED form of communication for business people of all types. From the basics of blogging, to the intermediate areas – such as social bookmarking, and article marketing, to the advanced techniques using auto responders and more, there's something for every affiliate marketer to put into motion.

The great thing about blogs is that people read them for fun and for information – in fact, blogging is one of the few areas of the internet that covers business, pleasure, networking and play.

They do for your company what face to face marketing could only do in the past – they provide you with a real, interesting connection to your readers – personalised contact, and information about your company that will allow them to empathise, and discuss your most important points, and anything that ties in with hot button topics and your business.

Blogs give your readers and consumers a chance, not only to read and connect with you, but a chance to comment and discuss with you, and your team, the information that you're sharing – allowing them to further relate to your message. And a consumer that relates to you is a customer in waiting!

Our guide covers the very basics of blogging – it skims into areas that you'll possibly never have heard of – and cover them so that you can employ them in seven days – or less.

Step 1

Starting a blog is as simple as finding a space online to write – and the time to write.

To start though, you'll need to work through a brief list of steps to create your space.

Before you even consider your blog though, you have to think about WHAT you're going to blog about. It's important to stop and think about your blog, before starting it because, to be quite honest, without purpose, blogs are pointless. And this pointlessness will dilute your message considerably.

So, you need to think about what you're writing and why. Consider your theme – and then build some keywords around it, because for the first little while, you should try to include at least some of them in every post. You'll get archived in all of the right places that way, which will lead valuable NON COMMENT generated traffic to your blog. You'll also be commenting on blogs similar to yours and hopefully, generating more traffic based on the links you leave.

You can choose your topic, keyword, and theme simply by considering what, in connection to your business you're an expert in. Once you've looked at that, you can decide whether it's profitable, or viable to pursue it. If not, look at a related area that you can cover – your blog should always relate to your business choices, and give you interested traffic. Having said that, your blog isn't a free advertising system and nothing more – you've got to remember that people will be turned off by blatant advertising.

Choosing your keywords

Keyword Research

Keyword research is relatively simple – you can undertake basic research at

https://ads.google.com/home/tools/keyword-planner/

You can use this to research your general keywords – and check on their general profitability, if you're using CPM advertising. You might not be – but most blogs make a residual income from AdSense or similar, and it's not something you should overlook, for your long term stratagem. Niche blogs can earn well.

Once you've found a profitable overall keyword, you'll need to check out your competition :

https://www.wordtracker.com/

Though considered less effective now – it's still a good tool for finding your competition levels. You'll be able to assess your competition – basically, you're looking for a niche that's either tiny, if it's narrow, or large, if it's broader. Your narrower niches can only support a tiny amount of blogs – whereas the broader your definition, the more your niche will support – but the flip side to that, is that you've got more competition.

Once you've worked out your profitability, and competition, you can also use the keyword search at Overture to evaluate your other keywords (and get an idea on where to start blogging from).

You can place that information in a spreadsheet for reference – or use programs like article architect to extend on your research (affiliate link for article architect)

Once you've made a list of your keywords – and paced them into a spread sheet, you can take your research a step further. Article architect does it for you, but if you've not got that piece of software, or a similar one that researches keywords, you can do it manually.

Open up both Google and Yahoo, and start plugging your keywords into it – at the top you'll see a listing 1 of (a number) – you can then divide your 'competition' number by the total of your searches (a number) – that will give you a rating for that keyword – and the keyword with the 'best' ratings are the ones you'll probably want to focus on.

Article architect does this automatically – highlighting the 'optimum' keywords – and there are other pieces of software will do the same.

The reason you're doing this is to see where your keywords will have the best chance of ranking – you'll be able to find the best place to 'position yourself' this way.

Keep those keywords handy – you'll need them when you start writing content.

Got your keywords? What do you want to blog about?

Once you've got your keywords, you'll have an idea, at least, of the profitable areas of your niche that you can take advantage of. You'll be able to choose an interesting niche – for both you to write in, and your prospective readers.

You'll find that you can narrow it down pretty easily based on what you've got on your keyword lists – and what YOU feel like you want to write.

While its important to work out what you want to do with your blog, based on your view of profitability, it's also important to remember that working based on keywords alone is a sure fire way to build an impersonal, and possibly unmotivated blog for your readers.

Step 2

Look at what you're ABOUT to do from a reader's perspective

One of the more important actions anyone creating or 'cleaning up' a blog can do is look at what you're doing or about to do from the perspective of average Joe reader.

Average Joe doesn't care about profitability. He doesn't care that you're optimising to make the most out of PPC clicks. He REALLY doesn't care that you've worked hard in getting your information into the search engine – and in front of them.

ALL he cares about is what they are looking for – and they are hoping that YOUR site is the site that will provide it.

Average Joe will remain on your site and read ONE POST in for anywhere up to 30 seconds. They might then click on your PPC advertising – they might sign up for your newsletter – they might read more of your posts (yes!) or, if your site doesn't live up to what they were expecting – what they were looking for, they'll click away, either back to the search engine, or to their next option from the search engine.

Blogging isn't just about eyeballs on your page – it's about eyeballs on your page, and comments in your inbox. People have to have a reason to come back, and the simplest way to ensure that is to ensure you've got a reason for them to WANT to visit your site again.

This stickivity is what makes blogging so tantalising- if you can get it right, your blog will attract Average Joe, Average Jane and all of their friends, because the best blogs get commented on in other places – and shared with others.

So, from a reader's perspective is your blog going to fulfil a) your niche and b) give your readers quality, quantitative content that will either strike a controversial or empathic chord with them, giving them something to comment on.

Give Your Readers What They Want

Studies suggest that there's up to a quarter of the internet reads blogs – that's a lot of eyeballs. And on top of that, another study suggests that there's two blogs founded every minute. Two blogs a minute is 120 blogs an hour – and nearly 3000 a day. Take that to its logical conclusions and that's a lot of blogs competing for a less rapidly increasing source of traffic.

More than that though, blogs are competing for a specific NICHE of readers – though its true that some blogs will pull in readers from search engines, blogs still don't have the impact of static sites – and the average internet user may not know HOW to search blogs.

Once you've got the absolute best information in your niche, you can be sure that you'll attract the right kinds of traffic, and that they'll attract MORE traffic by referencing you on their sites – bookmarking you, and more.

Blogging is all about the reader – ultimately, its not about how well you position yourself, or how strongly you optimise your site – though you can bookmark yourself, and generate a certain amount of traffic that way – the best sites have faithful readers that bookmark and discuss the site independently of ANY input from the site owner (you).

The best blogs are one or a mix of tips and advice, hobby or interest discussion, technique and connection. When blogging, if you can make a connection with your reader, then you've won most of the battle. 'Connecting' with your readers is as simple as being personable, and approachable, and giving people a chance to empathise with you.

Who is your reader?

Thinking about what your reader wants to see lets you work out WHO your reader is. Which you'll need later too, to advertise your blog effectively.

So who IS your ideal reader?

Do they have a specific interest, within your niche?

ULTIMATELY, when you know who your reader is, you can plan the creation of a blog that will fully appeal to any readers you attract. If you've planned on whom you're targeting, you'll find it far easier to write content that will continue to satisfy your readers, whilst giving you room to evolve and plan more content as you grow.

Got all of that sorted out?

Now you can move onto the technical stuff!

Step 3

Choosing your platform

There are several major platforms to blog on, but for simplicity's sake, we're only going to focus on three options: Wordpress (self-hosted), Wordpress (hosted) and Blogger. All three give you strong, steady options to blog from, and all three are easy to configure – and best of all, all three should integrate with any structure you've already created or are planning to create within your business.

You may find, however, that you can't integrate the self-hosted Wordpress with your site, but you should find that you can find a complimentary template on most good self-hosted Wordpress blogs.

Wordpress – self hosted

By far and away, one of the most popular options for anyone that is serious about their blogging, the self-hosted Wordpress option. You can install your blog anywhere on your site, and its completely within your control, which means YOU can choose what you'd like to have running – an important feature if you're looking to add the ability to do things like email the information to people, or polls. Or your own advertising in some cases.

By far and away, the easiest way to install Wordpress is via Fantastico – most cPanel hosts offer both Fantastico and the ability to install up to date Wordpress. Otherwise, you can find instructions online at **https://wordpress.org**

You can choose your own themes, your own plugins – and modify it in any way you see fit.

Wordpress (hosted)

Hosted Wordpress is a secondary option for anyone whose hosting won't support the Wordpress self-install options. You can grab blogs from lots of places, but places like **https://wordpress.com** won't allow you to run a commercial blog.

Hosted Wordpress blogs will only ever offer the very basics of WordPress blogging – you can't control the themes on offer, which means you can't choose a specific theme – unless it's already installed on the site. The same applies to plugins.

Blogger

Blogger is a Google owned blogging system, and is highly popular with non tech savvy people. It gives you a basic frame to build on – and is less flexible than either version of Wordpress hosted blogs.

However, Blogger is a great option if you really don't want to modify anything to do with your blog, other than the theme and possibly add some surface widgets.

Blogger also lets you archive your blog on your own site, giving you all of the benefits of self-hosting with none of the update headaches.

Ultimately, there are more software options for your blog – such as Moveable Type (Perl based) and Type pad (hosted, by the same company that offers Moveable Type and LiveJournal). Moveable type is not free for commercial purposes – another one that isn't free, but is a really solid blogging package is Expression Engine – again, you'll have to make sure that you get a valid licence for it, for the purposes you want to use it for.

What about CMS's?

I'm not recommending any of the CMS based systems, despite the fact that you can use them to build really nice, really strong blogs; you can't use some of the nicer features of blogging that you really need to take full advantage of, to get the most out of your efforts.

Most CMS systems don't have tagging protocols, track backs and pinging - though they have ways to leave comments per article or post, you'll find that they are lacking for full featured blogs.

All of the options will give you a blog that you can build a solid base from, but of course ultimately, where you want to build your blog, be it on your own website or via Blogger (to archive on your site) or hosted with another site, you'll have to stick with what you choose – purely for the fact that you're going to be promoting it – and the last thing you want is to move on after a couple of weeks cause you've played with the others and discover you prefer one over the other.

There is NO HARM in testing them all out first and getting comfortable, if you've never blogged – or haven't explored for a while. Wordpress (self-hosted) is easy to install 'vanilla' (no plugins or themes) via Fantastico – just follow the instructions presented and it'll install a simple Wordpress install in around three clicks.

Once you've gotten comfortable you'll need to decide on your theme – you'll also want to pick plugins for Wordpress, play with certain features in Blogger, and add widgets in other programs. We'll cover the plugins and other features for Blogger at the end of the book – for the moment, all you need do, now, is to find a theme you're comfortable with.

Picking a theme

Most people that found blogs have great plans – they want to write interesting content (that makes them money for their effort) and they want to be THE site that people come to for their information.

Most people don't consider what they want their site to look like though. Whether this is a deliberate oversight or if they just don't know what to do with their theme, it's probably one of the biggest 'beginner' mistakes that anyone can make.

Blogger comes with lots of pre-installed themes – or you can add your own CSS to it, to give it your 'unique' look. Its important to at least personalise any theme you choose be it on Wordpress(self-hosted) or Blogger – its not possible on hosted versions of Wordpress, or at least, not as easily. There are customisable options on Wordpress.com but they cost money and they are still aren't as flexible as you can have on your own site, so aren't as customisable as you really need to present a professional image for yourself and your blog.

There are many themes that you can choose from – and it can kind of be like decorating your first house – lots of fun, but very wearing!

Wordpress:

https://wordpress.com/themes
https://nicepage.com/wordpress-themes
https://athemes.com/collections/free-wordpress-themes/
https://www.templatemonster.com/it/temi-wordpress-gratis/

All of the above sites allow you to use their themes for free, though its well worth checking the licences – some are completely open – others are restricted simply to personal use.

You can also buy templates from professional designers – or look around and see who other people are using. It's a fair bet that your colleagues or favourite blogs will have designers to recommend highly.

Blogger

Unsurprisingly most Blogger template sites are actually hosted ON Blogger, so you've got a vast array of free blog themes.

https://sites.google.com/view/free-blogger-templates/

https://colorlib.com/wp/free-blogger-templates/

https://btemplates.com/

The final site also contains a lot of wonderful tips out with the scope of this guide, about how to add more features, such as web albums and forms.

Themes are easiest described as the thing that 'skins' your site to look different – more than that though, your theme controls ALL of the appearance of your blog – it's not just the wall paper on the walls, but the walls themselves in some cases.

Step 4

Blog content

Putting the cart before the horse?

Writing for the web isn't a case of collecting your ideas and then putting them online – and blog posting especially is a hidden and deceptively simple looking 'art form' all of its own.

Before you actually write one word of content though you need to think about what you're going to say. You should have your keywords organised into some sort of coherent list – and you should be weeding out the ones you're not interested in using. Once you've done that, you need to sit down and plan down your blog. You need to plan at least 20 posts and choose some sort of posting schedule.

Once you've planned your content, you can start writing your posts. In the case of WordPress, you can queue your posts as you are writing them, giving you the additional advantage of being able to post series and have them ready to go, without losing your flow. If you're using blogger, you should still write your posts as you can then simply copy and paste them into your blog on the day you want them to go live.

We always recommend that you stay at least three posts ahead of your posting schedule – that way, if you hit a dry spot, or find yourself too busy to post; you've still got 'emergency' content on tap, till you can re-evaluate.

What should a blog post BE?

Blog posts should follow one of a few formulae, but before you look at them – you should probably consider what they can and can't contain – there are a couple of 'no no's' in blogging.

First and foremost – your blog should be advertising light, if it contains any advertising at all. People don't want to talk about your latest and greatest advert – they want to read about your opinions and thoughts in your niche – they want to know that you DO actually know what you're talking about, and most importantly, they want to discuss, not be sold to.

This means that though your blog will do the job of promoting your product, you have to do it without being blatantly, obviously advertorial.

You CAN write about products – talk about why you're so passionate about them – their features, the things that make you want to use them – or the services, or problems they solve.

You also don't need to just WRITE – you can upload pictures, podcasts (audio), video, multimedia – in fact, the more interactive your blog is, without intruding on the experience of the average visitor, the more traffic and return visitors you'll get and the more comments your blog will garner.

Writing for the web

Writing for the web is an art form.

You need to use short sentences, with subheadings, usually one per paragraph – those sub headings should be bolded, to stand out, because studies have proven, without a shadow of a doubt that the majority of internet users, especially those with a lower technical savvy than usual, skim read.

They skim read because we've been conditioned to believe two things about the internet: there's a lot of good information out there – but it can be incredibly hard to find, even on 'trusted' sites.   Google's quality, page rank and duplicate content algorithms go a long way to helping to sift the dross from the perfect, but we're still left with people gaming the system, or worse, not being able to clearly state what we, ourselves are looking for.

Back to Average Joe for a minute. He doesn't know how to use Boolean operators, in fact, it sounds too complex maths like to be of any interest to him, and many internet users don't search for things as much as ask Google questions.

Keyword searching is a really good technique to learn, but for most people typing in short phrases, or whole questions, is the way to go, complete with punctuation.

Depending on the sophistication of the software in question, they might get exactly what they are looking for, but the same studies that suggest people skim read, also tell us that people really don't understand how to get the most from the internet.

It was best summed up in the X-files – the truth is out there – but where?

Skim reading users do have their advantages – internet writing doesn't need to be tight – just on one (tiny) topic. Blog posts can cover one tiny minutiae of a subject and then head back, stating it differently, another day.

There is one exception to this rule – when the situation or post doesn't warrant that style, don't use it. It's easy for someone to suggest that you blog using subheadings, but if you're blogging about yourself and your family, you might find it very hard.

Blogging is ultimately about YOUR BRAND and YOUR STYLE, so use it well, and you can't go wrong.

The most popular blog post formula

Blogging has fallen into several styles, like articles in newspapers and magazines. You can write and choose to use several different formulae, but ultimately, you have to find a way, and a style of writing that is comfortable for you.

The most common and most responsive way of blogging is 'problem – solution'. You take one common problem or current trend, or newsworthy topic and you 'solve' it.

Solving it can be as simple as providing your opinion, showing where you stand on any given issue, or it could be offering an actual solution to a problem many of us encounter.

Problem – solution or 'action – reaction' blogs are very popular with a vast majority of readers, but aren't without their inherent problems.

For a start, if you're 'solving' a current newsworthy item, although you are giving people a view of the fact that you are, in fact human, you'll also find that unless you are being very careful about expressing your views, you're going to upset someone, somewhere along the lines.

This can be a good thing – being of conviction in what you're saying not only gives you the authenticity that most blogs lack, for fear of stirring up trouble, but will also promote conversation – but not all of the conversation you promote will be positive.

You have to take the good with the bad and accept that no matter what you do, you'll always ruffle some feathers – just like in real life.

Another type of highly popular blog post is the review.

It's fairly straight forward to write a review post, but you've got to be careful. If it doesn't fit with the theme of your blog, you'll find that it actually damages your overall traffic. Your blog should always be laser focussed on the niche you want to talk about, and related areas to the niche. You can't go off topic!

Another type of post is 'a list' – lists of the ten most popular (x)'s.

(x) reasons why (y) is the only option/ a very bad idea

(x) reasons why you should/should not do (y)

(x) lifesaving hacks.

The highly popular blog, **https://lifehacker.com** is full of these tips and tricks – an article centred on solving a problem. The problem may not be implicitly stated, but instead touched on in general terms, but the solutions are always bang on the money, and that makes this blog a must read.

Its style is easy to emulate too. What problems does your niche have – are there several solutions (that you know of?) and can you express them in simple terms?

The final type of post that is very popular and easy to write is the feature – features can be one article, or several long articles, with links to each other. They should cover something important and be packed full of information. Keyword rich, you want your readers to come away feeling like they've really learned something, and search engines to come away with a whole new platter of wonderful content to add to their indexes.

The art of writing itself

Ultimately, you have to remember that though some blogs are founded for personal gain, if you're working on it to make any sort of income at all; you need to consider that your blog is a marketing project. You're either marketing the content, your company, or in some cases, yourself.

Once you've gotten your head round that, you'll also understand why you can't use slang, or make spelling or grammar mistakes, but more importantly, you'll realise that blogging might be the one 'voice' or face you present to people, so you'll need to offer a consistent, interesting brand.

There are specific, specialised types of post that work well with blogs from an internet marketer's point of view – like information about your company. Go beyond FAQ's and contact information – and share the nitty gritty about your operation. Make your blog readers feel like they are getting in on a secret of some description – or share something that wouldn't ordinarily be online – such as your motivation for going into business.

You can also recommend other marketers that you like, without appearing too fawning, if you're honest. Talking about experience is a sure fire way to improve on both your customer image, and your professional image.

You can also....

Use your blog to archive articles and other freebies for your company.

More importantly than that though, always ensure that you've got somewhere in your blog for people to sign up to your mailing list. Giving them the option to do that will also mean that you've got multiple traffic streaming to and from you blog, and though it seems odd to set up like this at first, people ARE more likely to sign up for your newsletter (with and without incentives!) if they like what you're saying on your blog.

As an extra bonus, you can 'tie' your blog feed to your auto responder, giving people the option of signing up to receive your posts by email – thus negating the need to come to your site until you post – we've covered that in the 'advanced' section of this book.

It has been suggested that there's a definite link between people that sign up for your newsletter, and people that comment on blogs attached to newsletters – and these people are the ones that are interested, interactive readers. They have a vested interest in commenting on your blog.

Style AND substance

Blogging isn't just about providing search engine content, and though its a great way to make connections with your customer base, the most important thing to remember is that shallow content breeds shallow contacts.

What this means is that if you're posting trivial stuff, people that are interested in little more than the trivial stuff will read your blog, and no one else.

Post about the 'meaty' stuff – and you're more likely to not only getting responses, but to gain responses that will help you further shape your content to fit your readers.

Though you will start out with a strong plan, and should try to stick to that as much as possible for the first few months (so as not to confuse yourself or waste the research you did in founding the blog) you should also consider the needs, wants and interests of your readers. Do THEY comment on more of one type of content? Can you write to fit the things they are raising?

Purely from a stylistic point of view, blogging works far better when you're using the active tense (Our newest division opened – we're putting the finishing touches to a launch) rather than the passive (our new division was opened – we've been working on a launch) – passive tense is both flat and doesn't contain energy. Its motionless, and doesn't give the impression of dynamism, which, when keeping a blog is very important.

Speaking of dynamic – ALWAYS be enthusiastic!

Blogging should never be a chore, and if it begins to feel that way, you really need to stop and question WHY.

Blogging is about sharing your passion, your enthusiasm, and your experience with others, and to do that, you've got to believe in what you're writing. If you don't, then how can you expect your readers to enjoy and comment?

If you love what you blog, you'll never work a day on your blog, in your life ;)

Step 5

Promoting Your Blog

Just putting your blog online is not enough. Once your content is off to that flying start (and its perfectly acceptable to found a blog and then backdate a couple (though, not too many!) posts to give your readers something to read. So over days 1 to four, you should have decided what to blog about, created and installed your blog, made sure you've got enough content to last you at least a month and posted it.
Now what?

Well, the long and short of it is, NOW comes the hard work – NOW you have to promote your blog.

Promoting your blog will put it in front of people. Fortunately, there's a myriad of ways to do it, but, unfortunately, they all take time.

Blog Marketing Ideas and concepts

You'll want to make sure that once your blog is developed and in place that its positioned perfectly to capture your market – in doing so you'll find that your blog markets itself.

To start with though, you've got to find your niche – the USP you want to target.

Defining your blog's USP is easy – what sort of reader do you want to attract, and what are they interested in? Does your blog cover it?
That's IT!

Once you've worked out your blog's USP, you can then plan where you want to advertise and approach readers – you'll also be able to track down competitors and colleagues in the arena that your blog. You'll need to know about them to know where best to comment!

Make Your Blog pull people in...

Your blog should, quite literally, mesmerise people and draw them in – interest them in reading about your opinions and information, and most of all, be completely on point for what they were expecting. Your blog should contain as much unique information as you can possibly manage, whether you've rewritten it from PLR or written your content from scratch – it should ALWAYS be unique. You'll avoid Google's duplicate content filter, and better than that, you'll get a reputation for not following the herd.

In the case of internet marketing, this does include ads about launches, but one of the biggest mistakes most bloggers (and mailing list owners!) are making is that they think that they HAVE to share the mailing information they've been given, as an affiliate.

This is a mistake because like seeing the same image over and over again, people will start to block out affiliate based ads – so instead of sharing what you've been given, verbatim, how about writing your own ads?

Its unique content and will interest people far more than flashy music or templates, but having said that, you do need to consider making your blog at least a little memorable. Choose a template that speaks to you on a professional level, but is uncluttered, unfussy, and most of all, interesting and easy to use. There's no point in using a flash template or a FLASHY template if you've got little to no clue how to make it work.

Making your customers aware your blog exists is a bit harder, but not impossible.

Most internet marketers have access to forums, mailing lists and more – so use them to tell people about your blog. If you're lucky, a 'big dog' marketer will see what you're talking about, and link to you – hint, talk about them, though don't say anything untrue! - and you'll probably get some spill over. These 'big dogs' might also consider running a solo ad for you, but you may have to pay for it, and unless you're in exactly same niche as them, or at least one that overlaps considerably, this may not be all that worthwhile for you.

More ways to let people know you exist.

Blogging is an emergent technology – you have to keep this in mind, because if its an emergent technology, so are the ways you promote your blog.

You can promote blogs via link exchanges designed specifically for blogs. There's several of them including:

https://blogcatalog.com
(in this case it only accepts blogs on the Wordpress platform)

Blog catalogues are probably a very good way to get a very small, but very targeted amount of traffic – usually around a similar level to submitting to places like

https://www.searchenginejournal.com/submit-your-site-to-yahoo-and-dmoz-directories/1440/

(a directory for everything online, edited by humans).

Blog link exchanges are less common, despite the fact that there's technology in place, on most every blog, to allow people to share important links, but so far, there's been very little in the way of 'automatic blogrolling' possibly because its so open to abuse.

There are sites though, that run link exchanges specifically for blogs. One of the less typical and highly popular versions of this traffic exchange for blogs is a site called 'mybloglog'.

Mybloglog as an internet marketing hotspot.

Mybloglog isn't JUST a traffic exchange – it provides 'a return on attention' – it is, in essence the bloggers blog tool. And for an internet marketer, its quite simply a community with leverage.

And as communities go, built around blogging, mybloglog is really quite cool. Owned by Yahoo, it does a great job of providing traffic, and growth to blogs.

And therein lies the rub.

You have to be very careful when using traffic exchanges to promote your blogs.

Most PPC based networks (unless you're lucky enough to run your own) frown on it – and some people have reported that they've been banned from ppc using it.

Even Yahoo's oddly.

Having said that, if your primary interest is traffic, you don't need to worry. mybloglog gives traffic until you're swamped. And its fairly targeted, as long as you categorise yourself properly.

Mybloglog's community is also a rather interesting place to hang out – you can pick up tips, tricks and find other blogs that are in your niche – again, you need to know where these people are, if only to know what your competitors and colleagues are doing.

Blogging is, when it comes down to it, a community 'thing' – you need a community around your blog for it to be a success, and on the whole, mybloglog provides the community aspect that most people need – at least to begin with.

OPB – other people's blogs

I've mentioned, while explaining a lot of this, that you should also know where your competitors are in relation to your blog.

Other people's blogs are also a great way to attract traffic – after all, they've already got people from your niche coming into their blog – the leg work is done – and the really big ones in your niche also have a nice secondary effect.

MOST blogs, when you comment on them, or comment about them and trackback (see the advanced strategies for more information on this!) will provide a link back to your blog, with your comment.

Sometimes its 'no follow' (a protocol introduced by Google et al. to combat spam) which means you don't get 'credit' in the search engines for your link back, but people can still click through to your blog. Its always of vital importance that if you're making a comment that you WANT associated with you that you include a link to your site. Each link has the potential for traffic, either coming to your blog to blast you for your view point (this is still good traffic, believe it or not – if the person cares enough to come over and challenge you, they may stay to read more) or to agree with you, which most times is where you'll pick up new readers from other people's blogs.

The people that agree with you, especially on controversial topics are automatically more likely to comment on your blog – and once someone opens a dialogue, they usually continue it.

That's not to say you should troll blogs to disagree with others. You shouldn't deliberately look for a reason to pick a fight on another blog – in fact, its usually good practice not to argue at all on blogs. If you truly believe the person blogging is presenting a 'fake' point of view, by all means call them on it. Lots of Big Dogs meet people doing that all the time, because its human nature to take a pop at something further up the food chain – but its important that you're doing it for all of the right reasons.

Though controversial conversations are the basis of strong blogging conversations, its also essential that you come away from them looking like a reasonable person, with understandable and approachable way. And as with everything else in blogging the keys to this are reasonable and approachable.

Passion is important, but tempered passion, and reasoned argument are usually the best way to attract people from controversial topics – after all, would YOU feel comfortable talking to someone that screams everyone else down?

Responding to Other Blogs

Controversy aside, there are some important etiquette points to pay attention to when responding to any blog post – or to comments on your own blog: Make sure you understand, fully, what the person is saying. You shouldn't respond to a comment in anger- it'll only lead to escalated tensions, and if something was said in a joking way, however unclear, you'll probably come off looking like the bad guy, even if that's not how YOU meant it. People perceive comments the way they expect the tone to be – so if its out of character for you, it will, generally look far worse.

Once you're ready to respond, you should stay on topic – or at least, start on topic, if you're responding on your blog. If you're responding in the comments area, remember that its a small area and doesn't allow anywhere near as many words as you can fit in a blog post, so if its a LONG response, you should consider taking it, instead to your blog. You should then always link back – blogger ad Wordpress both track these – bloggers calls them 'backlinks' and Wordpress calls them trackbacks (more about effective use of them in the 'advanced' section at the end of the book)

Ultimately, the person that owns the blog gets to decide whether to run your comment. You can't force someone to post your comment and harassing them, again and again, will only lead to you being banned, and possibly named and shamed. Unless this blogger is an unreasonable person themselves, this will only lead to damage.

The bottom line to this is that the more readers you have, the more traffic you have – the more customers you should generate.

Step 6

The social networking and bookmarking debate.

So far, we've touched on the basics of commenting, blog marketing and mybloglog – now we're going to go into slightly more advanced techniques for garnering readers.

Social networking and bookmarking has grown in popularity alongside blogging and though not all of them are designed to be used with blogging, most of them are.

Example Site :

https://digg.com

Digg is, quite honestly, the mother ship when it comes to generating traffic from social networking – you can be pretty much certain that if anyone makes it on Digg, they'll soon be complaining.

NO server is designed to stream the loads that people see, after becoming a top Digg – its quite likely that though most people hope and dream of seeing traffic like that, you'll experience it once and think twice about ever attempting it again!

Digg is a great place to gain readers from certain niches – its a 'geeky' site, a lot like Slashdot, and is designed to draw attention to the sites that are in those niches, with worthwhile things to say. They do, however, have a business category, which means Internet Marketers, with the right slant, can use Digg for bookmarking.

Digging someone is sort of like saying 'I recommend this' – its a global word of mouth script, and is very, very good. Every time someone 'recommends' or diggs you, you rise back up to the top of the front page, giving you a brief chance in the limelight. If you attract more attention there, you'll be dugg again, and again, and again, or you'll sink until someone else diggs you.

There is no time limit on Diggs – no statute of expiry. So its also a great way to get traffic to older posts – and probably most importantly, you can Digg yourself. You shouldn't use your Digg account only for that, but its perfectly acceptable to submit your own site to Digg, occasionally.

The community can't – really – be gamed all that well, because its so vast, but there are ways to cheat at every social bookmarking site – Digg is SO huge though that many people find they just get...buried.

Like every community, it is, in part about friendships – the gaming effect would be really easy if everyone voted for everyone else, but, to be quite honest, most people vote for the stuff that really interests them. So once you hook them as a reader they WILL vote.

There's also no harm (whatsoever) in encouraging your readership, as it grows, to digg you, to bookmark you on delicious, or to add you to other sites – there are plugins and widgets designed specifically for that purpose – just make sure your traffic is voting for the best of your material, and you'll garner even more readers.

The main thing about Digg is its like a snowball. Gain enough momentum and people will continue to vote for you and you'll keep popping right back up to the top.

Step 7

Tying it all up

The seventh day to blogging is a relatively short one – is everything you're doing, working so far?

You won't be able to evaluate traffic, but you should have a comfortable grasp of what you're going to be doing with your blog, and possibly a few fledgling commenters'.

From here on in you should be scheduling regular posting, and regular interaction on other blogs, in communities and forums, and of course, most of all, planning a strategy for continuing the building blocks you've started.

You won't know – yet – where the best bookmarking sites for you are – nor will you be able to decide whether your keywords are appropriate as yet. You WILL, however, know how easily you've found your first week, and you will be able to adapt your project overview accordingly.

You should also decide at this point, where you want to focus properly. Do you want to post daily – and can you commit to that? DO you feel posting less often will allow you to build a stronger, fluff free blog, without over committing? OR would once a week be enough?

Whatever you decide, after the first week or two, you NEED to be consistent. You should find a routine to settle into and then work towards continuing that schedule for as long as possible.

It IS possible to make money from a blog, but those blogs are at the top of their field, and this is simply because they are the best in their niche, blogs wise. As long as you aim for the best quality you can possibly produce, comfortably, you can't go wrong. It may take you a while to attract traffic, but if, in a month, you're still struggling to bring people in, you should review that side of your blogging.

While great content is the cornerstone of the best blogs – they also have a certain amount of focus on traffic driving. At critical mass (when that traffic brings in its OWN traffic) you can relax a bit on that side, but it takes a while to get there.

You should always keep an eye on what works, and what doesn't though, because eliminating that will leave you with a leaner, stronger blog than people that don't pay attention to these things, giving you a definitive edge over your competition.

And beyond?

One month on.

Is your blog outperforming your expectations?

Every marketing strategy needs reviewed every once in a while. You'll need to tweak, to adjust, and most of all, lose the bits that you're getting nothing from.

Step One: Keep Track of Your Blog Results

Tracking your blogs stats is as simple as ABC.

First though, you've got to work out what you want to track. Do you want to track your traffic? Do you care more about comments? How about what you're earning...

Primary goal – traffic

Keeping track of your traffic is as easy as finding a stats program you like and using it. There's a great one built into Cpanel called Awstats, or you could use

https://analytics.google.com

Either way, you have to understand how to read the statistics.

Awstats is reasonably easy to understand – the most important two numbers in it are the unique visitors and your page views. You might also want to see who is bookmarking you – in the sense of coming back to visit you using a simple 'bookmark me' function in their browser.

Bookmarking beyond the simple 'favourite' concept.

Favouriting a site, or bookmarking it, is the act of saving the URL in a list that you can then access from a menu in your browser. But in recent years there's also been another way to bookmark a site – and that way is interestingly, to drive boatloads of traffic to your site, if used correctly.

Its most important to remember that this form of 'bookmarking' was initially based on the browser based lists we keep on our own pc's – designed around allowing you to 'share' your favourites with others.

And then sites like Digg, Technorati and Delicious sprung up, giving people a broad range of ways to mark out the best items in another blog – sharing it, with everyone that's interested in the niche of the bookmarked blogs. If you're using social bookmarking, you should also try to keep track of roughly how well it's working out for you – how many 'diggs' you're receiving, how much traffic its referring in. You should be able to see that in your stats too, by looking for URL's that refer from the sites that you're bookmarked on. If your website stats are doing their job, they WILL track this.

Once you know how well your traffic is performing, you can decide which content is driving the BEST traffic. If you've got a goal for your blog, be it making money, referrals, or simply driving traffic to your other site, you can use your traffic (and affiliate stats/earnings) to find out which posts are drawing the most traffic and work on extending on those results.

One month in you should have several 'cornerstone' posts that define the whole concept of your blog – giving your readers several strong posts that give both the tone and nature of your blog. These cornerstone posts should be among your strongest performing posts, or you should work on making a couple of stronger ones. These cornerstone posts can also be used, one month in (to give them plenty of time to index in search engines), as articles in sites like **https://ezinearticles.com** – giving you even MORE traffic coming in from relevant sites.

Advanced techniques

Feed Burner

Feed Burner is a great way to add additional options to your site, not limited to subscription boxes, portable feed results, reposting of your information (for example, syndicating your articles is possible just by giving people your Feed Burner code. Their site updates automatically, and you control where they are clicking through to if they are interested in what you are saying in your articles. Its win – win).

Feed Burner was recently bought out by Google, giving you several amazing new options – including opening up their Pro services.
Most people use a lot of the Feed Burner functions, so its highly recommended that you grab your own account and explore.

Advanced techniques with Feed Burner also include the ability to 'fix' feeds so that they are readable, and track your feed stats.

Once you've set up your feed in Feed Burner keep the URL handy.

AWeber

If you've fed your Blogger atom feed through Feed Burner this will also work, but Wordpress has feeds that work well with one of the most amazing things that AWeber offers for bloggers, and one of the main reasons I use AWeber.

AWeber has a facility that allows you to attach your blog feed to your email list, giving you the opportunity to email your list the instant you update your blog. This is a great way to automate some of your posting process. And all it takes is filling in a form in AWeber, and putting a subscription form on your site. Not so advanced really.

You'll also be able to set up a template for your posts at the same time – you can choose one of dozens of templates that can compliment your site.

There is in fact, only one caveat to all of this.

If you post multiple times a day, you run the risk of annoying people – and if you don't post enough, your 'newsletters' may not be issued often enough. So you've got to set it up to post at regular intervals, which is where this gets slightly complicated.

Optimal posting is once a week – BUT...if you've got time critical information, this might not work out well for you.

So, you need to work out how to get AWeber to send out an email once a week – if your average posting schedule is three posts a week, set it up to post your information every four posts – add one to your week's post UNLESS you only post once a week – in which case, set it to send once per week.

You'll also still be able to send 'broadcasts' announcing any time critical information – and you'll STILL be able to set up your auto responses to your list – effectively offering you 'triple duty' on your autoresponders.

Other autoresponders may not offer this service so you'll need to check with them.

If your business is more list driven than blog driven, you can also take your list and post it to your blog. You'll need to find a plugin that works with your program – and this does not (as far as I'm aware) work with Blogger.

Trackbacks

There are more ways than one to pay regard to a good blogger – if you're linking to – or someone is linking to you, MOST blogs will track this.
Its called 'tracking back' – or backlinking in blogger – or, sometimes even pinging.

It is the art of linking back to a blog that you've read, and referenced – but more than that, its a way to get an effortless link BACK from a blog that YOU read, as long as they accept trackbacks.

Its an advanced technique, because you can't just 'trackback' to from any post – its important to choose only one, two or at a maximum, three blog posts to link back to.

When linking back, you have to use a special link, in the case of WordPress, its simply got 'trackback' on the end.

You use the 'regular' link in the post – this 'regular' link would be exactly the same one as you use to access the single post – you then put /trackback/ on the end of this, and place it in the box designated trackbacks.

As far as I'm aware, Blogger has no option to do this, but might automatically post them.

No matter what you do with your blog, you'll always find that you can get more traffic, more interest, and more eyeballs to your site with a blog.

And no matter how you work on your blog, if you follow our pattern, you'll find that in a month you can make a huge impact on your website.

"To Your Greater Success" !

Email List Building

(For Your Blog)

How To Generate Leads. Many Strategies To Grow Your Email List Quickly. A Step by Step Guide For Beginners To Launching a Successful Small Business.

By: Santiago Johnson Smith

(BONUS 2 – SECOND FREE BOOK)

TABLE OF CONTENTS [BONUS 2 – FREE BOOK] - EMAIL LIST BUILDING:

Description

Tired Of Looking For New Customers & Yearning For Residual Income Streams?

Discover How YOU - Or Anyone - Can Quickly & Easily Create Your Very Own Recurring Income Generating Asset Online...

Allowing YOU To Increase Profits From Your Repeat Customers While Building Your Own Expert Status & Credibility In The Process!"

Dear Internet Entrepreneur,

Perhaps you're here because you are still seeking the *right answers* for your Internet business and you need them fast... or perhaps because your business is still really struggling for success.

Let's work together on changing all of that today!

You probably already know the secret to creating recurring riches online... You know, the one that allows you to make money at will and pull in sale after sale, just like clockwork?

Yep, you have probably guessed it: it's having a responsive mailing list.

You can build your own database of prospects... and then build a relationship with them so that they *want* to say subscribed to your list.

You can remind them about your main product that you are selling on your web site... and invite them to return for another look. You can make important announcements so these prospects can visit your site **and then, sell them even more of your products!**

These are just some of the ideas, but you get what I mean, right?

"But It's Often Easier Said Than Done, Isn't It?"

Well, that's list building for you. It's only easy to do if you know the techniques that really work.

Quickly And Easily Build & Grow Your Online Mailing List For Maximum Profits!" And I leave NO stone unturned in this section... because I want you to be able to absorb and USE these valuable tactics right away!

Discover 6 totally different and unique strategies that you can easily execute right now and build your mailing list from scratch! It doesn't matter if you have only a few hundred subscribers or even 0 - these methods can be carried out right away!

What you get:

* A killer technique that can enable you to double or even triple your list building results using any of these tenderfoot techniques alone!

* How to get TARGETED traffic funnelled in from major Search Engines online FREE!

* How to use articles to build your mailing list and establish yourself as an authority figure in any niche of your choosing!

* How to earn decent returns from paid advertising online - I show you how NOT to waste money in lousy advertising PLUS show you how to identify paid advertising revenue that really works!

* What it takes to achieve MAXIMUM opt-in rates from your list building campaigns!

* How to drive in laser-focused traffic from popular Search Engines with little investment, MAJOR returns!

* How to use online/offline media to build your database of responsive prospects without having to risk being too "sales pitchy" and resorting to hype in the process!

* Create your vital credibility and then your mailing list through this popular vehicle as used by TOP marketing gurus from around the planet!

* And much more!

Chapter 1: Search Engine Optimization

A Short Introduction...

Thank you for investing your time in this special course, which is likened to the key to your list building success! List building is very, very critical to the success of any business online or offline. And it applies to your success whether you own a small, medium or big-sized business.

Brick-n-mortar companies invest a great effort in collecting prospective leads.

Network Marketers often begin with writing a list of 100 names of people they know. And as an Online Business owner, you should focus on building your Online Mailing List.

Now list building isn't exactly a riddle... as long as you know what to do, and how to do it. Incidentally, that is the aim of this book - to show you how to get started on building your mailing list using multiple, unique and different techniques that add TARGETED leads to your database at as low cost as possible. Yet you can profit wildly in the process.

As more than one technique is discussed in this book, you have my word that at least one or more techniques would suit you - or anyone. Of course, it would be wiser to practice more than one list building technique simultaneously to observe greater results.

Without further ado, let's move on with the first tenderfoot list building technique... Without a doubt, one of the most effective ways in which you, as a website owner, can set up a potential list of clients is to build an email list of those who visit.

SEO (Search Engine Optimization) Introduced By being able to better interact on a more "one on one" platform, you can quickly convert those who would otherwise simply browse around on your website and then leave, into potential sales and money in your pocket.

The profit potential does not stop there though, as with a well-constructed email list filled with people from all walks of life, you can even entice your subscribers to visiting your website more often than they normally would - setting you up to enhance your site's moneymaking ability even more through various advertisements.

So as you can see, the email list is one of the most important tools in any webmaster's repertoire and if you want your online business, no matter what it is, to be as successful as possible then you will need to spend a lot of time perfecting that email list.

Now, you are probably thinking that sure, an email list is great, but let's not get ahead of ourselves - there are many more steps to be done before we can actually start directly marketing to people on an email list.

SEO - Step-by-Step :

First, we actually have to get the visitors to our website before we can even dream of adding them to our mailing lists.

A few years back with the rise of popular search engines like Yahoo and Google, a group of cunning marketers, probably not unlike yourself, decided that the best way to get random people and potential customers to visit their websites was to take advantage of search engine technology.

They figured that if you could code a website and write content for it that designed with the sole purpose of moving that page's status in any given search engine to the top, then they would be able to receive far more visitors than anyone ever thought possible.

In today's web design world, the theory of search engine optimization, or SEO as it is often referred to, is an extremely popular topic among web designers and online business owners from all walks of life - no matter what they are selling or if they are even selling anything at all.

With so many competing websites in your chosen field or niche the only hope that you may have to rise above the seventeenth page of Google is to make sure that your website is as optimized for search engines as it can possibly be.

Because SEO is so popular these days there are hundreds of different websites out there that claim they have the answers to make sure that your page is among the top ten on all of the big three search engines: Yahoo, MSN and Google. However, if you take these tips and tricks on their own, you will quickly discover that there are far too many for you to take in. Perhaps the case is that everyone thinks they have the solution to the SEO problem - but nobody really does, so they just make things up hoping they will attract more visitors to their own websites. Therefore, when scouring the World Wide Web for all sorts of information on how to make sure that your website is optimized for search engines, it is a great idea to compare and contrast the information you find at one website with the information you find at others.

Comparing and contrasting is tedious though, so to get you started, we have already done a bit of the tough legwork for you so you can jump right onto the SEO bandwagon and get your email lists up and running in no time.

Search Engine Optimization Tips :

The first of our comprehensive SEO tips for those looking to establish their own mailing lists is to make sure that your website is as straightforward as it possibly can be.

Anything that deviates from the ordinary, whether it be Adobe Flash integration, crazy layout schemes or the use of dynamic URLs for certain pages under your domain can be disastrous to the budding web designer who is trying to take advantage of SEO for the first time.

Secondly, be specific with the keywords that you select for your website. Far too often, a person who is looking to get into optimization will select a perfectly good keyword but it will be far too general.

What you are looking for are specific keywords, keywords that are searched relatively often but lack the heavy competition of more generic keywords. After all, suppose you put "book" in as your keyword.

That's all well and good, but to be perfectly honest, your website will probably never compete with the likes of Amazon or Barnes and Noble, so be more specific. Consider something more along the lines of "antique book," "first run book" or something like that instead. Finally, be sure to direct your entire website to the optimization cause.

If you want to bring in the traffic (and keep potential customers around for a while) you will have to have great content. That is a no-brainer. But did you know that you can make other parts of your website work for you too? Yes, take advantage of adding your chosen keywords to the header portion of your HTML document, make the titles of your website contain the keyword too, and do not forget to use the "alt" image tags to proudly display your chosen keywords as well. After you think you have a fully mature search engine optimized website up and running, your next step should be to focus on your mailing list. Tweak and tune your content to make sure that it is good enough to make people stick around on your website and offer visitors something that will make them want to join your mailing list.

Promise to give people on your mailing lists essential updates, one time only offers, or whatever else you think is good enough to make them sign up to your email list. Often, the most creative ideas are the most successful, so go wild with your ideas and you will have a successful email list in no time.

Chapter 2: Using Article Marketing

How many different email marketing lists do you belong to? If your mailbox is anything like mine, then you probably have subscribed yourself to quite a few during your browsing sessions online.

Whether the emails that you get are from other businesses that may be able to provide you with goods or services that you simply cannot get anywhere else for the price, for musicians who you like to keep an eye on in hopes that they will visit your city sometime soon or from bloggers who have great articles in your eyes - your email box is probably filled to the brim with notifications that you subscribed to at some point or another.

Now that you are considering moving into the realm of the online business, it is high time that you learn to take advantage of the power of an email list and notification program.

Potential clients and random visitors alike love notification lists, as it keeps them up to date on what you've got going on without them having to visit your website every moment of every day.

People like things to be easy - and that is exactly what an email list is giving them - easy access to information on your website when they want it.

At this point in your career as a blossoming webmaster, you probably do not know too much about the whole web design thing. However, even with your potential lack of experience, you have probably realized that it takes a well-designed website with some killer content to draw people in and make them stick around.

While terms like article marketing and SEO may elude you, it does not take a rocket scientist to realize that you have got to have good, enjoyable, enlightening information on your website to make your guests want to stick around - and one of the best ways to do so is to be involved in an article marketing program.

So What Exactly Is Article Marketing?

Quite simply it is just as it sounds - marketing your articles and taking advantage of articles written by other people to bring traffic to your own website. Because of the definition, there are two very different ways in which you can become a part of the article marketing phenomenon.

Submitting or using:

Whichever method of article marketing your prefer is entirely up to you, although the former is much better way to attract traffic to your website and the latter should only be used in extreme situations.

Thanks to the wondrous power of the article marketing websites, there has never been a better time for you than now to become a better writer. Writing Articles For Business Marketing - You see, in order to be able to take advantage of the amazing marketing potential of submitting to an article marketing website, you first have to be able to write your own articles.

For some people who truly enjoy writing content all day long, this will not be a problem as they will be able to crank out great content in no time and flood the article marketing websites with lots of cool articles that everyone will want to have on their websites - easily getting their names out there so that they can start to establish a comprehensive email list of potential clients.

However, there is that problem that many people face who simply cannot draft an enjoyable document if their life depends on it. If you are one of those types of people, the road to establishing an email list through article marketing will be long and arduous.

Eventually, you will be able to write an article that you deem worthy of submitting to an article marketing website. After some time you may even get a few hits on it and a few unique visitors to your website because of it.

But how much time are you willing to spend on something that may only net you a couple of people on your email list? Instead, why not try hiring a freelance writer.

There are droves of them out there in cyberspace who will work for relatively cheap rates and provide you with decent content (and if you don't like what they have provided you with, you can always edit it).

Although many article marketing websites require that you write the articles yourself, if you have a ghost-writer do the dirty work for you, you can claim the article as your own and nobody will be the wiser.

Submitting To Article Directories :

Once your article writing is finished, it is time to submit your work to an article marketing website. After it has been up there for a while you will start to see people view it and you may even get a few downloads here or there.

It is the downloads that you are really looking for, as it shows that someone found it interesting enough to put it on their website using your name, link, and email address so that people will know who actually wrote the article in the first place bringing your website traffic. Below, you will find a comprehensive list of some of the better article sites on the Internet. There are literally hundreds of sites, but these are the ones you could start with.

List Of Article Directories :

Article City
https://www.articlecity.com

Article Finders
https://scholar.google.com

Articles Factory

http://articlesfactory.com

Articles Network

http://articlesnetwork.com

Constant Content

https://www.constant-content.com

Go Articles

https://ezinearticles.com

How To Advice

http://howtoadvice.com

Idea Marketers

https://www.ideamarketers.com

Morgan Article Archive

http://morganarticlearchive.com

The Ezine Dot Net

https://www.theezine.net

Certificate.net

https://certificate.net

Now, you can also use other peoples' articles on your own website if you must, but remember that you have to provide plenty of links to the original author's website - a risk that can possibly drive people away from your own website before they are able to enrol in your email list.

Getting people onto your email list through an article marketing plan can be tricky and arduous, but for the most part it is one of the more successful methods for establishing a good client base.

A lot of work must be done before you even think about posting that first article on an article marketing site, but once you are through with that all you have to do is sit back and watch as it brings in more and more potential customers to your website.

With each unique visit, there is another chance that person could sign up for your email list. And we all know that the more people on your email list at the end of the day, the more people you can sell to in order to maximize your profits.

Chapter 3: Paid E-zine Advertising

Building a comprehensive email list is one of the most beneficial techniques afforded to webmasters and online business owners these days.

There is perhaps no better way to establish a massive database of potential clients than through an email list that contains the names and email addresses of many who have passed through your site.

However, the problem remains that people must first visit your website before they are able to sign up to your email list, and even the most novice of us know that driving an abundant amount of unique traffic to our website can be a daunting task.

Luckily enough, there are many ways of getting the traffic that we all desire. Some of these ways are free but may take a bit longer to amass hordes of people while other methods require you to pay a fee up front but seem to work a bit faster.

Whichever you decide is totally up to how much you feel you can make in your online business and how much you are willing to spend in an attempt to gain as much traffic - and as long of a mailing list, as you possibly can.

Paid Advertising Explained:

Of the paid for methods of building your own email list and bringing gobs of traffic to your website, possibly the most successful is through paid e-zine advertising techniques.

The e-zine is a relatively obscure topic for most people, and chances are that unless you are really into marketing and advertising you have never heard the name "e-zine" mentioned before now.

Essentially an e-zine is basically an electronic magazine that is published by a particular website.

Different than a mailing list, an e-zine is usually tightly linked to a particular topic or subject, so that everyone who has access to a particular ezine is interested in that one topic.

There are unique e-zines for just about anything out there from how to build a successful website to how to find the best shoes to where are some of the best destinations for people who like to travel by boat.

The possibilities for different types of e-zines are endless, so the first step in any paid e-zine advertising plan should be to find and research the different types of e-zines that will fit into your site's niche.

Sourcing Out For The Best Paid E-zine Advertising:

Once you find a particular e-zine that you feel is the right media for your advertisements, you should contact the owner of the e-zine and see if he is open to the idea of you sticking your advertisements in the e-zine itself.

If the e-zine owner is open to the idea of paid advertising, then you are good to go and you should start creating some advertisements immediately.

On the other hand, if for some reason the owner of the e-zine is not interested in sticking your advertisements in (for any price) then you should simply move on to another e-zine that is also well suited to your business.

Creating Your Own Advertisements:

Now comes the tricky part for any potential paid e-zine advertiser looking to enhance the membership of their budding email list - creating the advertisements themselves.

The ads you make will have to be more than simple content if you want to unleash the full power of a paid e-zine advertisement.

Remember that hundreds, thousands or sometimes millions of people will be viewing the e-zine with your advertisement in it, and if you want a decent majority of those people to actually click your link, visit your website and subsequently sign up for your email list, then you will have to be especially clever with your advertisements.

Even more so if you find that there are multiple advertisers competing with you in the same e-zine issue.

Many people at this point will probably think that their best shot for successful paid e-zine advertisements will be to advertise exactly what their website does, and why someone should pay any attention to it.

Unfortunately, while this may be decent for some people, it is a practice that has proven to be unsuccessful for those looking to build an email list. After all, if a person knows exactly what they are getting from your web service, then why would they want to visit your advertisement if they weren't interested in your services?

That is all well and good if you are selling only one particular product, but you want to craft an email list.

So instead you need an ad that will piqué their interest in what you offer something that will make them want to visit your website, sign up for your email list and come back for more again and again. This is the only way that you will find yourself able to maximize the payout from a paid e-zine advertisement if you are trying to create your own email list.

The Maximum Opt-In Conversion Rate Solution The solution to maximizing email list subscriptions through the use of a paid ezine advertisement is to give the people what they want - something for free or your services in a risk-free offer.

Whatever it is that you offer them for free is totally up to you, and in all honesty it docs not really matter so long as you give only a rough idea of what your potential customers are getting for free in the advertisement.

You can give away anything from a free article to free research to a free one week subscription to whatever services you are trying to peddle. Just make sure that you let everyone reading the advertisement that if they visit your website they will be entitled to something cool totally free of charge. Now, just make sure that the e-zine advertisement you have created points directly to your email list sign-up page, tell your visitors that they have to enrol in your email list to receive the free gift and you are all set.

Oh, and be sure that at some point you do actually follow through with giving the people who sign up for your mailing list or you may have a few angry people in the following days. And there you have it, the start of your brand new email list as only paid e-zine advertising can provide!

Chapter 4: Pay-Per-Click Programs

If you want your website, online business or blog to be as successful as it possibly can be, and to be honest - who doesn't? Then what you need is a comprehensive mailing list with names and email addresses of all sorts of people to market your products or services to.

Since most visitors to any given website do not make a purchase on their first browse, it is of the utmost importance that you keep track of as many visitors as you can with an email list. That way, you can more directly market to them later on and convert that marketing energy into sales to generate you profit.

Making the hard sale the first time out is extremely difficult, so use an email list to let the buyers come to you - and then grab them when they are ready to purchase something from you.

The email list marketing tactic works for just about any kind of online (or brick and mortar) business, whether you are selling products, doing custom research for people or writing articles that they can use on their own websites. In order to build an email list that you can later use to solicit your products, you first have to drum up some visitors to your website. This is actually the most difficult part of the task because there is so much competition out there for just about any website.

Even if you think your website is so unique and different from anything else out there, I can almost guarantee you that you will have at least ten other sources of direct competition for your same market - making it harder for people to pick out your website when there are others that may be just as good (in their eyes) as yours. Although search engine optimization and article marketing are viable methods of generating traffic for your website, if you really want to rake in the traffic to build a huge email list, you will have to consider using a pay-for method like pay per click advertising or paid e-zine advertisements.

Sure, neither of these marketing techniques come cheap - but if you can add even a handful of the visitors you get from these campaigns to your email list, then a pay for advertising method will be totally worth it.

Pay-Per-Click Exposed!

Thanks to the success of the search engine business in the past few years, the pay per click advertising method seems to be the best payoff for someone looking to generate traffic and build their own email list. Because so many people frequent search engines like Google and Yahoo each and every day, pay per click advertising is the perfect way for you to get unique visitors to stop by your website - even if search engine optimization techniques have not been able to bump your website up to the first page yet. So, if you are interested in gaining the best benefit for your buck in terms of visitors to your website, then paying Google or Yahoo each time someone clicks on your ad is well worth it.

How It Works:

Each and every time someone clicks on your ad, you will have to pay a small amount of money to the company you purchased the ad space with, but if you are turning most of those visits into sales or valuable additions to your email list, then the fee will be well worth it.

Google is one of the biggest names in the search engine business and their ability to bring in visitors to all sorts of different websites should not be taken lightly.

With well-placed Google pay per click advertisements, just about any web business owner can turn his downtrodden website into a moneymaking bonanza in a matter of weeks.

Thanks to their ingenious AdWords program, Google will be happy to give you a plethora of pay per click advertising space on the results page of peoples' searches to advertising sections on other peoples' websites.

Yes, with a contract with AdWords you can be well on your way to getting visitors left and right. However, as with all things that seem so great, there is a catch with Google AdWords - you have to work long and hard on choosing the right keywords for your website.

The special algorithm used by AdWords only shows a few relevant ads based on keywords, so if you are unsuccessful in choosing the right keywords for the most effectively targeted ads, then you will be left with far fewer visitors to your domain than you though.

The other promising choice for those looking to get into pay per click advertisement as a way to get visitors to their website for email list purposes is to use Yahoo's Search Marketing (formerly known as Overture) service.

Since this service has been around much longer than Google's AdWords, it is much more robust in terms of what you can do with it.

While AdWords is much more focused on targeted advertisements, with Yahoo Search Marketing you can actually target your ads by different criteria - not just by the keywords you have chosen to use. This gives you as an online business owner much more flexibility over who gets to view your ads and when they get to view them.

Now that you have been acquainted with the top two names in the pay per click advertising marketplace, you should be better prepared to make a decision about how you want to go about attracting visitors to your website.

With pay per click advertisements, you do not have to worry about spending money frivolously on ads because you never have to pay anyone until somebody clicks on the ad for your website. Furthermore, with both Google and Yahoo, you actually get to name your own price for how much you pay per click - making pay per click advertising a feasible method of generating website traffic even for those webmasters on a tight budget.

As one final tip for anyone looking to get into pay per click advertising as a way of building an email list, make sure that your advertisement is linked directly to your email list signup page, as you cannot expect people who have visited your website via an ad click to browse around for long.

Chapter 5: The Value Of A Press Release

Building a successful website can be tricky business - especially if you have plans to make that website the crux of your income statements each year.

After all, with so many other websites out there that are probably selling the same or similar goods and services as you, what is there to set your business apart from the pack?

One simple answer should be the contents of your website. People like a nice, clean design for the sites that they frequent and they like to have plenty of enjoyable articles or copy to read that is genuinely interesting to them.

If you are able to supply those two fundamental features you will be well on your way to making your online business thrive. But what if you want to take that extra step to make your website into a moneymaking machination?

There is one simple tool that you can employ if you want to ensure that you will get more people to purchase from you - create an email list that potential customers and current customers can sign up for.

The mailing list allows you to do something that most stores wish they could do: attract visitors and then market products to them on their schedules so the hard sale does not seem so hard to swallow in their eyes.

Even with a small email list you will have a much higher rate of sales than if you were to forgo the email list all together, so what do you say - perhaps it is high time that you create one for your website. Unfortunately we cannot go around and simply collect random names and email addresses to add to our email lists, so it is up to us to first generate enough traffic for our website and then convert those visitors into email list subscribers.

There are tons of different ways in which you can get traffic to come – some ways, like pay per click advertising cost you some money while other like search engine optimization are totally free so long as you know what you are doing.

However, both of these techniques are totally passive. Try as you might, it may take you weeks or months before you actually see any of these techniques come to fruition as actual inquiries on your email list.

Instead, if you want to grab the proverbial bull by the horns and rake in people by the droves right away then you will have to do something a bit more drastic.

Bring In Press Releases!

That something is a tried and true technique that has been employed by businesses of all types for centuries. Known as the press release, you can use this method to drive people to your website almost instantaneously the moment someone picks up and publishes the release.

At this point you are probably thinking that such a technique is too good to be true and would be impossible for a lowly online business owner like yourself – but the good news is that anyone can draft a press release and submit it to many of the major daily publications, both online and print based. All it takes is a little bit of time and some know-how of what you need to include in your particular press release.

Drafting Out Your Press Release:

The first aspect of a press release that you need to concentrate on is the actual content of that release itself. Nobody wants to read some drab, boring press release - and certainly nobody will want to publish it in their periodical, so consider jazzing it up to include a lot of content that people who would be interested in your website would want to hear. Include facts, figures, statistics and even plans of action for what you and your business plan to do in the future in an attempt to get people to check out your website.

Remember: no sales pitch, too! People expect something newsworthy from you. While you should make the content as interesting to your potential customers as possible, it is important not to lie, since chances are that your potential clients will check up on you over time to make sure that you are wholly backing up what you say in press releases with what you actually do. Also, when writing the content, be sure to address your possible clients personally instead of addressing them as some vague demographic as far too many press releases tend to do. This will make the reader feel more at home and will likely make him or her more inclined to visit your website.

Secondly, if you plan on submitting your press release to mostly websites who will publish it, then you should try to optimize it for search engines as much as possible.

Remember that the more aligned your press release is with certain keywords the more it will be read by people who could be your potential customers and subscribers to your new email list, and the better it will be for your business in the long term.

Please though, do not overuse the keywords you have decided to focus on, as it will make for a very dry, boring and uninteresting press release that certainly will not allow you to get the maximum number of visitors.

Finally, once your press release has been written and edited, you will want to find some spots to post it. I recommend these (but there are many more if you 'google' the term):

https://www.prweb.com
https://www.newswire.com
https://www.imnewswatch.com
https://www.pr.com/press-releases

Be sure to get into contact with places that you know will be able to distribute your press release to the masses, but also try and find some avenues of distribution that take advantage of RSS or Atom feeds. Using RSS or Atom will allow your press release to be sent directly to the masses like the top headlines for the New York Times or Google News and is a great way for your business to take advantage of technology in the pursuit for a massive email list.

So there you have it, the basics for using a press release to gain as many visitors to your website as possible. Since you are looking to establish an email list from many of those visitors, be sure to have the link from your press release pointing to your subscription list page, as you do not want people to dawdle around on your website and lose interest before they sign up for your email list. Do this, and you will quickly find that your website will be successful in much less time than you ever thought possible!

Chapter 6: Using Special Reports To Kick Start

Your Campaign Marketing is about contacts, and in today's business world, emails are as valuable as just about any contact you can have. The key, though, is not just to have a list of emails; it is to have a list of qualified emails that you can turn into clients and profits.

Certainly getting a list of qualified email contacts sounds great, but how do you do it? There are a number of ways to get qualified emails, but one of the most effective ways is through the special report.

When used properly, the special report can give you and your business credibility while helping you to build an email list of qualified potential clients.

Take a look at the information below and you will quickly be on your way to building your business through an email list created from a special report.

Creating a Report About Your Subject:

Perhaps the best way to encourage perspective clients and customers subscribe to your e-zine or email list is to provide them with relevant and useful information. Your special report allows you to provide something of value (information) to your prospects without discounting your product or giving anything away.

Before you can start to use your special report, you obviously will need to create one. This is the most important part of the process, because if the report is not put together correctly, its effectiveness will be compromised even if you do everything else exactly right.

Start by considering niche topics that will benefit your prospective clients. If you offer real and useful information, those who read the report will be more likely to opt into your email list in hopes of gaining access to more useful information from you down the road.

If your report is not useful, prospects will be less likely to read the report and even if they do it may not result in the email opt-in even 'sticking with you' and with whom you are hoping to build your email list.

Secondly, research your special report heavily and make sure that your information is rich. Good content will bring opt-ins while bad content will just disgruntle prospects and leave you with a bad report and no emails.

Finally, proofread and edit heavily. Your content should be smooth, well written, and easy to understand. Good information that is easy to understand makes you look good.

On the other hand, good information with lots of errors and that is difficult to understand will may make you look inept. Have several sets of eyes look over your special report before you move on.

Turning Your Report Into A PDF Document:

The next step, once you have written your special report, is to have it converted into a PDF document. PDF files have a more professional look and can make you look technologically savvy to your customers.

What's more, they will look exactly the way you designed them no matter what the hardware or software is that the recipient uses. Converting your special report into a PDF document is simple, so the amount of work you put in versus the payoff is profound.

There are a few ways to convert your file into PDF format, and one way is to find a reliable and free online converter (Adobe.com has one) or you can download a software product to use on your own computer. Using your favorite search engine, you can find numerous free software applications that will convert any printable file into a PDF file. If you are only doing a few special reports, this is the fastest way.

I recommend:

https://www.primopdf.com or https://openoffice.org for the job, but there are several others, as well. There are many options out there, so do your homework and find the one that works best for your business.

The important thing here is to make sure you get a clean conversion and that your special report looks professional and just the way you designed it.

Circulating Your Report:

You have created a special report on a topic that you know about and that pertains to your target clientele. That is great, but now you have to make sure that they are actually looking at the report.

If nobody reads your report, it obviously won't do you any good. So then how do you get your special report circulating and working for you?

First and foremost, make sure it is well known within your company. It should appear on your website as a download and your employees should have links to the download location on their email signatures.

This will give your existing clientele access to the special report and anyone with which your employees have contact: a nice start.

The second way to circulate your special report is to write shorter content that will appear online where your prospects are looking.

Write a small article that leads to the information in your report, add a link to the report at the end, and post the articles on content websites and even message boards. Spread the word through the industry that you have something of value for free.

Finally, create a flier or other print advertising for your special report. Include the location (a link) for the special report and make your flier available at conferences, conventions, and any other event where you may encounter potential clients. Getting the word out every way possible will assure that plenty of eyeballs are finding your report.

Building an Email List from Your Report:

Once you have a useful report with good content, and once you have properly marketed that report so that it is in front of potential clients, you need to get emails from them.

The email list you are about to build is the main reason you created your special report in the first place. So how do you build an email list from your report? If you have put together an effective and valuable special report, then your clients will want to give you their email. Your job is to make sure there is a way for them to do that.

Within your special report, offer opportunities to get more information from you by opting into your email list. Offer an e-zine or other information to potential clients who do so.

Provide links to your company website on most if not all pages of your special report. At your site, make sure opting into the email list is easy to do, convenient, and quick.

If your target sees something he or she likes, it should be convenient to get to your site and to sign up for your email list. Remember that the report needs to stand alone as both an informative special report and as a marketing tool to help you collect qualified email leads.

This is important as you allow the report to be resold and passed along by others in the industry.

A Valuable Tool:

As you can see, using a special report can be a great way to build your email list. What's more, you will find that there are many things you can do to make your special report an ongoing aid in the maintenance and continual building of your list.

Just remember to make the content good, the report valuable, and the opt-in process convenient and you will have a qualified and reliable list in no time!

This Ends Part One...

This pretty much sums up the basic techniques of list building. While there are obviously more advanced list building techniques that you can practice and use for your own, I thought you should know that many a top marketer are making it big online today using even some of these "basic" methods to build their list... to a great extent!

You now know what it takes to build your mailing list from scratch, and I would advice you to test every one of them to see what works best for you. This is because every individual is different.

Therefore there are some methods that would work especially better than the other for you. Are you ready for the 'intermediate list-building' training section now?

Chapter 7: Compound List Building with Resell Rights

As you may well know by now from the last chapter in Ultimate List Builder's Course, creating special reports is a great way to market your business.

You can use those reports to build your credibility, raise the awareness of your company, and acquire qualified lists of emails for potential clients.

In order to truly spread your special report around, which is how you get the most benefit from it, you should look into granting resale permission for the report.

Once you have written your special report, you have to find a way to make sure that people are actually reading it.
After all, getting people to read your special report is the only way to reap the other benefits of writing one.

As you will see, there is a lot to be gained from resale permissions.

In addition to that, it is easy to get started once you have written your special report. Finally, you will see that your email list may just be the biggest winner in the resale permission game.

What is Resale Permission?

You may have heard the phrase "resale permission" before, but it is possible that you didn't know what it meant.

Basically, if you grant resale permission on a special report you wrote, you are giving another person or company permission to sell or distribute your report and collect any profits for themselves entirely.

While that sounds like a great deal for the person to whom you grant permission, it is also a pretty good deal for you and your company.

Of course, first you have to understand how to do it.

How to Give Resale Permission:

Giving resale permission in and of itself is not difficult, but you want to make sure you do it the right way. Remember that you want to make it easy for your special report to get spread around. That means that you need to grant your resale permission the right way.

The best way to get started is with an opening statement that outlines your resale rights terms. Now, for some resale rights, you can offer up minimum resale prices, restricting free giveaways, and even restricting membership site usage.

However, if you are trying to spread a special report to build your business and your email list, then you should consider making your resale rights simple and easy to get.

The easier it is for someone to acquire the rights, the more likely they are to take on your report and start selling and giving it away. When you are trying to expand an email list, you need to make sure that you do add one resale right permission restriction. You need to make sure that the main text of your special report stays unchanged.

That will ensure that links and references to your website or company and thus assist you in growing your list. Overall Benefits of Granting Resale Permission For Your Special Report.

When you choose to offer resale permission on your special report, you can gain a number of advantages. For one, by granting resale permission, you are encouraging others to spread your report. That means more eyes reading the report and about your company.

Secondly, offering up resale permission gives you credibility. As other read the report and it is being resold, you become more of an authority on your subject and, by manner of extension, so does your company.

Finally, you create a viral situation. When you offer easy to get resale permission, you are basically enlisting a large number of people to spread your report one way or another. That just helps the word spread that much easier.

Email List Benefits of Giving Resale Permission:

What, though, does this all have to do with expanding your email list with qualified potential clients?

Simply, when you wrote your special report, you should have done so with proper wording and links so that your opt-ins would grow. With such links, references, and other referrals coming from your special report, you are looking for a way to get that report in front of as many potential clients as possible. So by granting resale permission, you are creating a way to get your report in front of more people.

The more people you have looking at the report, the more people you have getting the opportunity to look for more information with your company and the more likely you are to get people adding their names to your email list. This will help your email list to not only grow, but also to grow with qualified leads. As you can see, there is a lot to be gained by writing a special report and granting resale permission to others for it.

It is one of the most efficient strategies you can use to get your special report in front of as many people as possible. Remember to start with a report that actually has value.

In addition, make sure it directs people to your company website as well as your opt-in email list in order to build a better list of qualified potential clients.

Finally, give permission the right way. Do not overcomplicate things by putting a lot of restrictions on the resale rights. Instead, make it easy for people to acquire the resale permission and they will be more likely to take it.

Remember, you are trying to get your report to spread. You are not looking to make a profit on the report by itself.

So once you have that understanding, you can just allow people to spread your special report to all those potential clients and members of your email list.

Thus if you are looking for a way to spread your special report, check into the granting of resale permission.

You will be glad you did it.

Chapter 8: Using The Ad Swap

Whether you are writing an E-zine or building an email list, your clients are important. Have you already exhausted all other means of getting more email addresses? You may want to consider using Ad Swaps.

This is a way for you to not only to increase your client base, but also gain more revenue from other sources. You may find that something as small as swapping ad's with different companies will give you the boost you have been looking for.

So What Is "Ad Swapping"?

This is actually exactly what the name implies. You swap your firm's ad with another firm's ad. Finding an Ad Swap group is as simple as using your favorite search engine. There are many companies out there that are interested in Ad Swapping.
Swapping your ad with another company can greatly increase your chances of gaining more subscribers. When you swap ads with another company, you will be displaying their ad instead of your own.

This means that your ad must be short enough to work with the company's email layout, but also be informative enough to grab the attention of the reader in hopes to directing them to your website.

Ad Swapping is smart advertising. Many times when individuals are browsing the internet, they may not know what they are looking for, but those that are already subscribed to an E-zine or other list already know what they are looking for.

Using Ad Swaps Correctly:

By correctly choosing the right company to swap Ads with, you will greatly increase your use base. This is because the readers are already interested in what they are reading and see that the Ad pertains to what they are reading and also that it is recommended as a reputable site by the person who supplied the original email.

A simple Ad Swap can bring in double the amount of people that you have now.

Before you even consider swapping your Ad with another person, you need to create a one-line description that will really make readers want to click on your Ad.

The "Ad Headliner" is the single most important part of the Ad. Without it, you are not left with much. The Ad Headliner should not be very long but should contain enough information that grabs the reader's attention enough that they want to visit your Ad. This is the same as Internet Ads.

If there is a lot of text you must read before you figure out what they are trying to bring to you, you most likely won't click on it. For this reason, keep your Ad Headliner short and sweet but powerful.

Sometimes a few words will work best, its up to you to decide the right length that is informative without being long-winded. There are many different companies out there and it's important to make sure that the Ad you get in return will be fit for your client base, and vice versa.

One of the most important aspects to consider when you are looking to swap ads with any other person is how well their content relates to yours.

This just means that if your clients expect information about computer hardware, they aren't likely to click on an Ad that is about horse racing equipment.

This is not to say that everyone interested in computer hardware isn't interested in horse racing equipment, but at the time they are reading your E-zine, they may not really have that on their mind.

The topic of the Ad does not necessarily have to completely pertain to your Email, but it does need to be related. One other point to remember is to find out how many users the other person interested in the Ad Swap has.

Since you are interested in gaining new members, then it is in your interest to only swap Ad's with another person who currently has the same or more number of users. Of course, if you have only five percent more users than them, you can still give them a chance.

Just remember that you are interested in gaining new members, and if your Ad Swap partner has a fewer number of members, then your odds of gaining new members drops significantly.

What if you cannot find a company who shares the same interests to Ad Swap with? One solution to this problem might be creating a survey for your customers with a wide selection of topics for them to choose from.

This will help you understand what other interests they share, and can help you make a smarter decision on who to trade your Ad with.

back from all of your customers, you can safely choose one of the top interests and know that you will be doing your part in relaying traffic to your Ad Swap partner.

Choose your topics wisely though. You don't want to have your topics cover a gigantic area of interests, because finding a company that needs an Ad Swap partner with your particular interests may not want to trade with you if your material pertains to a topic that differs too greatly from the one they cover.

Offering your customers between Twenty to Thirty different interest topics to choose from will give them a nice selection, and make things easier when it comes time to find an Ad Swap partner. Joining an Ad Swap group can greatly increase the number of members you currently handle. It is one of the best ways to get more subscribers to your E-zine or other subscription email service. Be sure that you research each person who you are conducting the Ad Swap with as their content will be displaying to all of your subscribers and you are the one responsible if they supply you with a broken link. Be sure to write a few ad headliners and choose the one that is both minimalist and descriptive.

Without an attention-grabbing Headliner, an Ad Swap is useless. As long as you are sure to check over all of these points you should be on your way to conducting a successful Ad Swap.

Chapter 9: The Magic of Give-Away Events

Building an email list is one of the best ways to advertise the product or service that you are trying to market. This will keep your efforts focused on your target audience instead of to a broad range of people who may not need or want to do business with you.

For example, if your business deals with home improvement information and products, you would not likely appeal to someone who is living in an apartment.

The main purpose of building a large, active email list is to bring in a sizeable amount of active readers who are looking to you for good deals and benefits.

Successful e-zine creators often credit their good fortune with hosting Giveaways, or contests as incentive to get people to join. Of course, once they join they will expect to receive a well-composed and beneficial newsletter or else they will likely choose to unsubscribe.

A new business might not be able to afford to give away free products to subscribers in the beginning, especially without the knowledge of how successful the newsletter will be in bringing in actual profits.

This is why it is a good strategy to find at least one reliable affiliate who you can either trade products with, or that is willing to give you a wholesale price.

List Building Through Give-Away Events:

Before you approach anyone in search of partnership, you should be fully organized and have a sample newsletter ready to present to them.

Be confident and show them that you have the drive to put in the efforts that it will take to make it work. It may take patience and friendly persistence to have anyone agree to take on a risk involving finances.

However, this situation could be very beneficial for both parties. You will have the means to get a customer base built and, if they can supply you with their products to give away, they will build a good reputation and increase earning potential.

If you don't know where to begin looking for a business affiliate, try looking for a successful business of any size that is in the same product category. This could help you bring customers to each other.

You may not be comfortable asking for money or products, but you also have the option of trading equal parts of your products with theirs to give away to subscribers of your e-zine. They may choose to do the same, which would help both of you. Neither of the parties will lose much money considering low production cost to the manufacturer.

Using this strategy to bring in customers will have you making the money back in no time. A simple outline of what to do to find a partner is as follows: propose your strategy for building an e-zine newsletter to potential partners, show them a sample newsletter to gain their confidence, and use your skills of persuasion discuss ways that you could make the most of each of your products and help each other's business.

If they are hesitant and don't seem interested, move on. Anyone who has the ambition to start this type of venture will be able to find a partner who is just as eager to work with him or her.

Do NOT immediately advertise your Give Away.

It is important to wait until you receive the products that you will be sending out.

A formal contract should also be agreed upon and signed because they are a common practice in the business world. Decide when would be the best opportunity to give away a free product to subscribers.

If you do it at the time they sign-up you will risk having people sign up just for the gift and then canceling their subscription.

One way to ensure that your list grows, and remains active, is to require that membership is at least one month old before they can apply for the free gift.

Another alternative is to have a monthly drawing for the items you are giving away. That will keep readers of your e-zine entering each month for the contest.

This will give subscribers incentive and they may even help you by referring friends and family to join. Being aggressive in this situation will not hurt your reputation.

If you already have a great web site, don't hesitate to advertise the Give-Away exclusive to mailing list subscribers on every single page. It can be placed in a spot on the page that will not interrupt the flow of the page, such as the bottom or top corner.

Do you offer a site subscription?

Add a check box to the sign up page offering to automatically add them to the email list also. The free gift should not be the only reason they choose to sign up.

Offer a link to a sample of the newsletter so that potential customers can see the benefits and incentives that they will receive in each email.

You have to be ready to work hard to make people happy and keep them interested in what you have to offer. The double opt-in practice is important to anyone who is building a large mailing list. Anyone with genuine interest in becoming a part of your list will be willing to confirm their request to join twice.

This is your opportunity to remind them to add your address to their white list so that it is not filtered out with spam.

Using only single opt-in signups will bring in a large number but the quality of the list will definitely suffer.

You will either be filtered as spam or have to deal with a lot of un-subscribing from those who were never interested in what you have to offer.

Keep up the maintenance on your list.

Don't be afraid to ask for feedback from your active readers on what they would like to see more or less of.

This will let them know that you are genuinely interested in their business and satisfaction.

A Give-Away is a proven effective way to get a list started, but it is up to the creator to keep the list as active as it is large.

Chapter 10: Investing in Co-Registration Leads

Too often the key to your business working successfully is how much traffic you can drive to your website.

The type of product or services you offer can sometimes limit traffic.

This means not only do your potential sales suffer but so does the growth of your business. One way to improve this traffic flow is co-registration.

This means putting opt-in check boxes on the page where your customers register.

Co-Reg & Opt-Ins - They Go Hand-in-Hand:

Opt-in boxes are places that your customers, or even just those who visit your site, can check to say if they are willing to receive information on similar products, services or e-zine publications.

This allows you to build up an email list so that when you have sales or introduce new products you are able to get the word out to potential clients quickly.

Building mailing lists is an important part of running an online business. But, it is something you cannot necessary do all on own.

There are companies who can help you build mailing lists that will reach customers that will potentially be interested in what your site has to offer.

There are companies who will sell you co-registrations leads to help you build that all important mailing list. But before you agree to buy from them you must be certain that you will get exactly what you need. There are some basic guidelines to shopping around for a good co-registration service. To begin with, the company must guarantee you that the names you are being given are genuinely opt-in names.

The last thing you want to do when trying to bring in customers to view your offerings is to use names that have been collected without the customer's agreement and authorization. Then you also want them to guarantee you that the names have been generated recently.

Co-Reg Tips:

The age of the leads you invest in is a crucial factor. Names that were picked up a year ago will not likely be of any use.

People change their email addresses regularly when they change jobs or move. And, over time their interests change, as well. The products or services they were looking for which are common to your business may already have been bought.

That is what makes 'old' lists an even bigger waste of money.

The other thing to consider is price. The cost of co-registration lists varies from company to company so shop around until you find what you think is the best deal. Do not use price as the only factor, but use it as one of the factors. You want a company that will offer to you everything you need at a reasonable cost. Whether you are building your mailing list to draw people to your e-zine, announce new products or get new names for your monthly newsletter a service that offers you good co-registrations lists will save you time and a lot of work.

If you want a list that can bring you hundreds of names doing it yourself could take months. Getting them from a service cuts that to a matter of days and lets you get back to growing your business. There is no other lead generation resource better through the Internet than this.

If you are looking for a source of co-registration leads finding them on the Internet is not difficult. But you must try to find one that will offer you what you need.

The service at

https://smallbusiness.chron.com/coregistration-marketing-24798.html

seems to have a lot to offer to their potential clients, as do the folks over at List Opt. When checking out any list service, make sure that they offer is a guarantee that you will be satisfied with their products. Also be sure that they offer lists that are generated the correct way; with no contest lists being used to trick respondents into allowing their names to be taken. And it's VITAL that all their names are opting.

They will have co-registration lists that are aimed solely at that one area. This may be any form of product or service. One service that sells co-registration lists like this has them aimed particularly at those who are interested in Internet marketing. Their claim is that those who are on their lists are eager to find ways to make money on the net. So, if that is what you are offering on your website their co-registrations lists are for you. They can be found at Nitro List Builder. This particular company also offers larger lists than most others. They talk of the availability of lists that have from twenty to one hundred thousand contact names. Like the other one they promise their lists will be fresh ones.

Many of the co-registration sites that sell email leads are particular about what kind of businesses they will work with.

They will stay away from hot businesses, gambling sites or sites which reflect an attitude of hate against others. This shows that they are trying to make aim their business at others whose businesses do not hurt anyone.

They are careful to ensure that there will be no duplicate names and that all the leads you get are current. This is a very important aspect of co-registration leads and one that all services that sell these leads promise you.

You can always expect to get a few email addresses that have changed but if you wind up with too many dead leads you should contact the service you have bought from and demand replacements. If the number of dead leads is high they should honor your request. Some services will give you an extra one or two percent on your order to help ensure that you get the right number of goods leads for the money you have paid. Prices vary greatly on co-registration leads. You can pay anywhere from thirty-six dollars for one thousand names to three hundred dollars for twenty thousand names and many possibilities in between! You're Almost Finished With the guide Part Two... There you have it! Both the basics and advanced list building techniques are now as good as at your fingertips. Note though, that you require some substantial list and/or experience to use some of the advanced list building techniques discussed in this course, while others can be done just almost immediately. All in all, they can prove to be very powerful list builders if mastered correctly. It is my sincere wish that these techniques can help you expand your mailing list and in doing so, expand your Online Business Empire even further. See you at the top! (When you are ready for the "hardcore" level, let's get started with the guide Part Three... the last edition in the series... just scroll down!) Bringing Your Online Business To The Next Level Welcome to the last sequel in the Ultimate List Builder's Course series, where you will discover some of the most hardcore list building strategies as used and practiced by TOP Internet Marketers and gurus from around the planet! Now I am going to confess that it's not going to be necessarily easy to execute any one of these Master's Level of list building techniques, as they certainly require more practice backed by experience to leverage on them.

But it is a worthwhile learning journey as these list building techniques has been responsible for income breakthroughs of many an Internet Marketer, some who brought in thousands, potentially tens of thousands of red hot leads in a short time span, some literally overnight! I won't stall you any further as I could almost feel your excitement. Let's move on! Scroll down for chapter eleven... and learn more methods to help you build your list.

Chapter 11: Recruiting an Army of Affiliates

If you are an Internet marketer, one of the keys to a successful business will be your ability to bring potential customers to your website.

The best way to do this is to find a way to build large email lists of these potential customers. One of the most common strategies for doing this is purchasing opt-in co-registration lists.

An opt-in list, as you already know by now, are those where the customer has checked a box on a site saying that they are willing to receive information through their email for different products.

Building, or buying, these email lists are what will make the difference to a successful Internet marketing business. It does not matter what you are offering on your site, products you want to sell or services you are offering, if you do not have the traffic to your site you will not make money. IMPORTANT! You should not purchase lists that are not recently generated or that are not opt-in generated. If you do then you will not add to the success of your business but will find that too many of your leads are cold and you have spent money for very little, if any, benefit to your business.

Affiliate Programs Exposed:

Another way to drive traffic to your site is to become part of an affiliate program. This can be done either by joining an affiliate program that is already showing signs of success or by making one yourself.

Joining Affiliate Programs:

Joining an already established affiliate program has several benefits.

Obviously the first one is that the program is already up and running and so there is less work for you to do and less time to wait for results from the program. You would need to search the Internet and locate affiliate programs that are related to what your product or service is. It would make no sense to sign up to any program if the topic is not close to what you are doing. This does not mean that you should be concerned that you are signing up in a program that is run by your competition.

In reality any affiliate program you join that properly reflects what you are marketing on your website will have other members who potentially are your direct competitors.

This does not matter. Customers will shop around. If what you offer is a better product or service, with better financial considerations the customers will come to you.

This gets others to help increase your business prospects. What you want to do is get the affiliate programs to work for you. In this way you create your own email lists, use ones that you have bought and bring them all together through an affiliate site, which will not only generate potential customers for you but can potentially earn you money as you send customers to other sites.

With affiliate programs, if you join them, then you get commission on their sales. This can be a nice perk as you work to bring traffic to your site.

Creating Your Own Affiliate Program (RECOMMENDED!) If on the other hand it is your chose to create your own affiliate program you have the advantage of being able to have it exactly the way you want. Just remember as your affiliate site grows and is successful your will be paying commissions to others on your sales.

This is true of our own program or one you join. This practice is a reasonable one since what you are doing is attempting to get people to your site and the more methods you have that you can use the better. Think of it like having salespeople in your store. You would have to pay them a commission or salary to sell your goods. This is more or less the same thing.

With your affiliate site you will need to generate interest for the potential customer to come there and for others join. One way to do this is to have lots of interesting information for potential customers to read. These are usually in the form of articles.

These articles should be related to your product or service, but not all of them should be solely with the aim of selling. You will find that sometimes a less pressured sales pitch will attract more customers. Still you want to provide lots for them to read that is related to your Internet business.

Another way to bring people to your affiliate's site is make sure these articles have lots of keywords. Keywords are what the average person uses when they are searching for something on the net. For example, if a person is looking to buy a rattle for their friend's new baby, they will likely write in the words baby rattle, but they may also put in the words baby gift, new baby, baby toy etc. So, the more words that you can put in your articles that will come up in their search the more likely they will visit your site. You do not put the keywords in just once but several times so that your articles will come up nearer the top of a search. When creating your affiliates program you will want to have an interesting lead in for others to use. Pay per click is another option for you through your affiliates program. These can be highly successful but are often difficult to monitor. They can easily be abused by others to generate an income for themselves while not truly sending any traffic to your website.

Remember your affiliates program will generate your own email leads. As long as they are opt-in generated you also have the option of selling these lists. But most importantly you have them available to use along with any lists you have paid for to generate more traffic to your site as well as to help the customers who have joined your affiliate program. A common piece of advice to those who are trying to start up an affiliates program or just get an Internet business rolling is once you have discovered something that works, stay with it, then repeat it and continue your success!

Chapter 12: Leveraging on Joint Ventures

Electronic communications are the simplest way to sell your good or service today. As such, it only makes sense to continually expand your targeted email list.

But how do you go about doing this? One of the easiest ways is by networking with partners who also have email lists. However, if you are going to be effective with this, there are several things you have to keep in mind. Here are some tips on how to find partners with the tight type of email lists, and also how to use those lists to the mutual benefit of both parties.

Where To Look For Potential Partners One of the first places to check for potential partners is among professional associations. Often, you can build rapport very quickly with others who are in some way connected with the same general area of expertise that you offer with your service or product line.

Of course, you are not looking to partner with anyone who would be in direct competition with you and your company. But chances are the professional association membership will cast a wide enough net that you can find at least a few professional partners who are engaged in offering goods or services that are complimentary to what you have to offer.

As an example, let's say that you offer discounted international long distance services. You happen to belong to a professional organization for persons who are part of the telecommunications industry.

In addition to long distance, this would also include audio conferencing, web conferencing, and video conferencing. You might find it a very good fit to approach an audio conferencing provider about sharing qualified email listings. The potential for them to pick up some new conferencing customers is certainly there, and you may also find plenty of changes to snag some new corporate long distance clients as well. Along with professional associations that relate to your industry type, there are also the broader organizations, such as city and state chambers of commerce.

Membership in these types of organizations can easily pay for itself with just one good lead on someone to partner with. This will often involve making sure you attend chamber events, especially mixers.

The focus here is not necessarily to find persons who deal with services that are part of your industry, but persons whose clientele represent who new markets for you, and vice versa.

For instance, at a local chamber event, you strike up a conversation with a sales director for a national legal form supplier.

As part of their customer support, they have a monthly e-newsletter they send out to their clients. As it happens, you currently make your living selling transcription services, and have quite a few legal firms in your client base. While your two business interests may appear to not have much in common at first glance, there is plenty of reason for the two of you to talk.

You could certainly endorse the use of their forms supply business, and they in turn would be able to open doors for you to additional attorney firms, arbitration services, and others where transcriptions are key to the working day.

Trade magazines are also a great way to get leads on organizations that you may want to partner with and share email lists.

In order to do this effectively, you may want to look closely at the composition of your current client base. What industry types are represented in your base?

Which sectors of your client base are generating the most revenue for you on a monthly basis? Are there existing parts of your client base that you would like to grow?

Answers to these questions will help you determine which of the many different trade and industry magazines you want to subscribe to, and use as leads in securing venture partners.

Other Details in Joint Ventures Pay attention not only to the features, but also any columns that mention companies in passing. In like manner, see who is advertising in these magazines.

You may find some great leads among the ads. If there are classifieds in the back of the magazine, do not discount finding a good lead or two among those classifieds as well.

Of course, you do not want to forget online resources. Just about everyone is online these days in one form or another. Look for web sites that are dedicated to the type of good or service that you offer. Often, there will be links off those sites that can lead you to potential venture partners.

Many of these sites will have message boards that can also connect you with other persons who would be interested in sharing qualified email lists as part of a joint project. While these may take some time to cultivate, in the end they can provide a big payoff.

Don't forget the possibility of utilizing your own web site as a way to attract potential joint venture partners as well. Depending on your business model, it may be quite appropriate to create a page that is meant to attract potential partners in a join email sharing campaign. Provide some basic guidelines that have to be met, such as proof that the list is qualified, that it is a current and usable list, and that no one is included without express permission. Then provide a way for anyone interested to contact you about moving forward. It cannot be stressed enough that you make sure to only work with persons who can provide a legitimate email list of persons who have requested to receive email transmissions.

There are far too many email lists on sale these days that are antiquated or compiled from sources that would do nothing to help you reach your target audience.

Whether you meet a potential joint venture partner face to face at a chamber event, or make your first contact via a message board or a response to a query on your web site, you must set the standard.

Important JV Tip:

Make sure that you only deal with people who have the same level of ethics and respect for potential clients that you have worked long and hard to cultivate and establish.

Failure to do so will mean lost time and resources, few if any new clients, and most likely loss of some of your clients as well. Pick your partners carefully, however, and you will open up all sorts of opportunities to broaden your client base and increase your revenue stream.

Chapter 13: Executing Product Launches

As any good businessperson knows, nothing is quite as exciting as launching a new product or service. One of the best ways to have your new offering hit the ground running is by using a resource you already have in place to get the word out to interested parties: your customer email list.

Product Launch For Hard Hitters Utilization of your email list should begin long before the actual launch date of the new product or service. A savvy approach is to begin using the electronic communications to begin building up some interest in the new product.

As an example, let's assume that you do a monthly newsletter to your client list. Several months before the launch start inserting teasers into the newsletter.

Even something simple like "Not sure what to get your best friend for Christmas this year?

In September, we will tell you." Of course, you may want to be more direct and try something along the lines of "You told us you want it.

And we listened. Announcing Easy Web, our new web conferencing product, coming in August."

Of course, every month you will include a new tidbit about the new offering.

Use the space to extol the advantages of your offering over those from your competition.

Along with the teasers, build up to a feature article that goes into the background on how the product was developed and what influence existing customers had on the final design.

Customers love to know you listen, even if many of them never send you any ideas.

Pre-Launch:

As the time for the launch draws near, you may want to do some promotional work among your email listing as well. Offer premiums such as discounts to any existing client that can get someone who is not currently a customer to attend a demonstration of the product and who subsequently signs up for the product or service.

Among your client base, why not offer a short-term free trial, as well.

The point is to give your existing clients a chance to try your new offering, decide that they like it, and that they will be coming back for more.

Happy customers are some of the best word of mouth you will ever have, so if they like you and your new offering, they will be more than happy to promote you to other organizations.

In addition to using your regular e-newsletter to publicize the advent of your new offering, you may also want to do targeted emails from your email list.

Targeted emails would involve dividing your email list up according to industry type and preparing the text of an email that would point to applications of your new offering that are of special interest to that part of your client base.

As an example, you may have a large percentage of non profit associations In your client base. You know that your new offering could help them keep track of participation in fund raising projects they conduct.

Focus on that point, explaining how your offering can make the job easier and more accurate.

Critical Launch Success Factors:

It is important to note that you will not get a very good response if you do not do two things. First, you must send several well-timed emails about your offering between the time you make the first announcement and the actual launch date. Far too many people think that one announcement does the trick and there is nothing more to be done.

The fact is the matter is that you want to use your email list to build interest for your offering as the launch date approaches. Depending on your client base, a monthly email might be just fine. If you think you can do so more often, than give it a try.

You want to keep people informed, give them ideas on how to use your offering, but you do not want them to get tired of seeing emails from you and decide to opt out of your list. Find that sweet spot for contacts and you will be able to use the list effectively.

Also, it is not a matter of using material versus sending out individual emails. By all means use both. Chances are that your clients will take note of one or the other, but not necessarily both forms of electronic communication.

Of course, you want the emails and the newsletter content to compliment one another.

In fact, you may want the text of your email to refer back to the content in the newsletter, and vice versa. Keep everything consistent and very upbeat.

Along with getting out information on the potential applications of your offering, you may want to invite your client base to participate in some sort of a contest, with the prize being something that would be useful in the home or office.

However you choose to construct the contest you need to make sure of two things. First, it is imperative that you be able to verify the results.

Secondly, you should offer a prize that will not create any undue hardship on your company. You want it to be attractive, but not something that will potentially create a situation where you would not be able to meet your obligations. Of course it makes sense to only offer a three-day, two-night cruise to the winner if you can afford to do so.

Launching Your Product:

Don't forget to follow up the launch date with some more updates and invitations to try out the new offering. Continue to spotlight the launched service or product in your e-newsletter and in email communiqués to your client for at least four to six months after the launch.

The potential for them to share your announcements and feature reports with other people will not end on the day of the launch. Keep the momentum going and you may pick up a few more customers.

Your email list is a valuable piece of property. It is important that you responsibly use it to keep your current customers happy with you and your offerings, as well as let them know of new innovations that can make life easier for them.

At the same, time, it can be a wonderful way to involve your clients in the process of securing new customers who can benefit from a working relationship with you. Make sure your customers always know how much you appreciate them and you will be able to not only maintain but also continue to expand your email list every time you have something new to offer.

Maximizing Your Mailing List Profit Points:

Having a solid mailing list is one of your business' greatest assets.

Many of us know that the single most powerful selling tool we have is the good word of mouth we get from our existing customers. The fact of the matter is that your customers can help you to grow your business in several ways, as you find ways to up-sell them on other means of helping you help them grow their business.

Here are some suggestions that will help you articulate to your customers how you can help them grow while you are maximizing the profits that you get from your mailing list and e-zines.

Sell Advertising Space To Your Clients:

Chances are that at least some of your clients are involved in selling goods and services that would be of interest to other customers on your mailing list. So what if you were to offer some really competitive advertising space in your monthly electronic magazine?

This one simple offer could begin a whole new revenue stream for you, using a resource that at present does not provide any direct profit. In order to keep things as simple as possible, you could specify the format of the ad and also offer sizes that would be very easy to include, such as quarter page, half page and page size advertisements. Just as with any ad service, you could offer short term and long term rates for advertising in the newsletter, which would mean a steady revenue stream for you over the long term. Along with the newsletter, have you thought about offering the contacts in your email list the ability to place ads with hot links on your web site? You could create a whole section of advertising that is just for your client base.

As for pricing, you could set up a basic monthly rate, and offer discounts off that for commitments of six months, a year, or two years of advertising via your web site.

Assuming that you send invoices through regular mail, you could also create a lucrative revenue stream by advertising to contacts on your email list the ability to include advertising flyers in all your mailings.

Of course, you would want to pieces to fit nicely into standard business envelope and you would want to make sure you kept the number of inserts to a minimum. Nevertheless, you could create a steady flow of cash from even this type of endeavor.

Another form of advertising you could offer to your clientele is to include a onetime feature article in your monthly E-zine.

The article could include an overview of the history of the company, vital information about their core product line, or information about an upcoming new good or service they will be launching soon.

This feature article option could be offered with a guaranteed minimum word count as well as a bold header, for a flat rate price. Of course, you could also offer a sliding scale based on a fixed rate per word instead of the flat fee. This would allow your client to opt for a longer article, if they wish to do so.

Affiliate Programs And Your Email List:

The simple fact of the matter is that no one is successful with an affiliate program without owning a good solid email list. Since you already have a list that meets those qualifications, why not put your email list to work and make some money with affiliate programs?

Here Is What You Need To Do:

The genius of opting into an affiliate program is that you get to expand the types of goods and services that you offer to your existing customer base without having to invest anything into development, facilities, or production.

Someone else has already done all of that. By entering into an affiliate agreement, you tap into that resource, act at the mediator, and rake in profit off every unit sold.

One of the first things you will need to do is collect data on available affiliate programs. A quick Internet search will probably lead you to quite a number of potential programs that would be of interest to you.
You may also uncover a source or two that will provide you with quick overviews of hundreds of affiliate programs that are actively looking for persons just like you.

Make notes of anything and everything that you think could possibly be of interest to you. One thing to note here is that you will be able to find plenty of affiliate programs that will work just fine with your own sense of business ethics.

While there may be some programs out there that offer products that you would prefer to not be connected with, do not worry about limiting yourself. The breadth and depth of affiliate programs is such that you will have no problem finding plenty to chose from. After you have made your initial swing through the lists, is it time to begin matching up your interests and skill sets with what you understand about your own clientele.

As you look at each of the affiliate programs that have caught your eye, think in terms of what your customers do for a living. What products or services would be likely to compliment what you already sell, or at least be of some interest to those that already know and do business with you?

You can sign up for all sorts of affiliate programs, but if they are not going to excite those who already know you, then what is the point? Make sure that any affiliate program you sign up with has the potential to generate additional income from your email list.

Next, you want to do some checking on any affiliate program that you are sure is a good fit for you and the customers on your existing email list. What will you be looking for?

Find evidence that the program is stable, that it delivers what it promises, and that the majority of the folks who are affiliates are happy with the way things are going. Where will you find this information? On the Internet, of course.

Use your Internet browser to conduct a search for comments on the affiliate program of your choice. You want to locate as much feedback, both positive and negative, as you can manage.

No organization is going to be without its detractors, so don't let some negative comments turn you off immediately. How well an organization responds to the need to resolve an issue with an unhappy client says as much about it as having customers who do not experience problems.

What you do want to be aware of are any trends that indicate the affiliate program is misleading in some way, that it fails to live up to its promises, and that it consistently has a history of leaving affiliates in the lurch.

When you find ample evidence of that sort of behavior, then you know it is time to forget about that program and move on to the next one on your list.

Once you have identified one or more affiliate programs that you feel good about representing, then the next move is to let the folks on your email list know what is going on. Prepare a press release announcing your decision to open a working relationship with your new partner.

Outline some of the reasons why you have decided that these affiliates are a good match for what you already provide to your customers. You may want to include some bullets that demonstrate some reasons why your customers should look at your new partner(s) very closely.

Make sure that you have a link set up on your web site that will function as a portal to your new partner(s), so you can get credit for any business your clients do with any of your partners is credited to you.

If you have an E-zine that you produce on a regular basis, promote the products of your partners right along with your own services.

Keep the name of your affiliate partner(s) in front of your customers through the use of both email and your E-zine, as well as making sure there is a link to your partner on your web site.

Along with opening up new revenue streams by using your email list to promote this new affiliate relationship, you also can make sure that your existing customers have the means to pass on your information to their associates.

This can lead to the expansion of your opt-in email listing, additional demand for your own services, and increase revenue from your affiliate relationship as well.

Always Remember To Market Your Own Services One of the reasons you have such a great email list in the first place is that people have come to know you and trust you.

You've sold them goods and services before, and they have liked what they got both in the way of product and in the way of customer care.

Your job is to not only maintain that positive relationship, but also to build upon it. Upselling is the term that is normally used for the process of promoting goods and services to your existing clientele that they have not yet tried out. In many ways, this is much easier than trying to start with a new lead. There is already a history between you and the buyer, one that has demonstrated a good working relationship up to that point.

Chances are that your client will at least devote a few minutes to whatever new product or service that you want to introduce them to. It is your job to use the resources at hand to make sure that courtesy of giving you a few moments turns into a sale.

When it comes to email announcements, make them big and broad, but keep in mind that not all people utilize HTML setting for their inbound email.

For that reason, you may want to rely more heavily on the content and less of using graphics to spotlight a new or existing service.

In order to get the most our of your email announcement content, you will want to observe a few basic rules. First, make sure that the content of the email announcement is focused. Do not try to cover too much ground at one time.

Keep the content in line with the purpose of the email, which is to promote one particular product in your line.

If availability is pending, make that clear right up front, including the date that the product will be available. Outline at least three possible applications of the product that, based on your knowledge of your customer base, will appeal to a majority of them. Close with contact information to learn more about the product, including a link back to the page on your web site that features the product.

Second, make your email announcement can be easily scanned by your audience. Many people will glance over your email and then move on.

You can diminish that occurrence by having the announcement broken down so that key points will catch the eye of even the most casual reader and impel him or her to go back to the beginning and read all the way through.

Using headers and bullets are an effective way to make your announcement more scanner friendly, and will help hold the attention of the reader.

Last, make sure the email announcement is simply that: an announcement. The communication is not meant to function as a sales brochure, nor is it supposed to be an exhaustive study of the new product. It is meant to spark the interest of the reader and provide them with just enough detail to compel them to want more information. Generally speaking, if you can keep the announcement under 500 words, you will manage to keep the attention of your audience long enough to make your point.

In Conclusion… As the last section of the series in the Ultimate List Builders Course draws to an end, remember: your email listing can help you to generate additional AND substantial ongoing revenue for your Online Business. By offering advertising space on your web site and in your E-zine, you provide customers with the chance to reach a whole new audience, one that already trusts you to steer them in the right direction.

The use of affiliate programs creates opportunities to build on the relationships you already have with everyone who has opted into receiving electronic communications from you by offering them a wider range of products and services. Last, your email list provides you with a bank of persons who are already receptive to doing business with you, and will often be very happy to know about any new goods or services you are offering to them. With each of these three examples, and especially if you allow them to overlap in the way you utilize your email list, you have the opportunity to greatly expand your revenue stream, as well as broaden your client base.

To Your Ultimate Mastery Of List Building & The Maximizing Of Your Profits!

To Your Complete Success!

Resources:

Besides the links throughout the course, there are a few other favorite resources I'd like to share with you. I've used them myself and so I can confidently recommend them to you for your business.

Marketing & Business Tools You'll Need:

Payment Processor:
2CheckOut is my favorite

Clickbank is only for digital products but is good, too PayPal is a good free alternative to get started out Hosting:

HostGator is a place for hosting multiple domains very affordably.

Domain Name Registrar:

Ifastnet.com offers excellent service & pricing plus some other extras you may need besides your domain names.

Autoresponders:

All of these are good solid (and necessary) products...

AWeber

GetResponse

ListMailPro

FollowUpExpert:

MyAutoresponderPro

My Favorite List-Building Resources:

Click Funnels

Nitro List Builder

List-Opt's List Builder

Awesome Membership Site Script:

Amember works great for an affordable, easy member site script!

Positive reviews from awesome customers like you help others to feel confident about choosing this book. Thanks very much !

The End (BONUS 2) Second Free Book : "Email List Building"

By : "Santiago Johnson Smith"

DISCLAIMER AND TERMS OF USE AGREEMENT:

The author and publisher of this course and the accompanying materials have used their best efforts in preparing this course. The author and publisher make no representation or warranties with respect to the accuracy, applicability, fitness, or completeness of the contents of this course. The information contained in this course is strictly for educational purposes. Therefore, if you wish to apply ideas contained in this course, you are taking full responsibility for your actions.

Every effort has been made to accurately represent this product and it's potential. Even though this industry is one of the few where one can write their own check in terms of earnings, there is no guarantee that you will earn any money using the techniques and ideas in these materials. Examples in these materials are not to be interpreted as a promise or guarantee of earnings.

Continue to the next page...

CPSIA information can be obtained
at www.ICGtesting.com
Printed in the USA
BVHW012311040521
606339BV00018B/1487